10670209

TORONTO PUBLIC LIBRARY
JUL 2 6 2011
NYCL - BU

Related Books of Interest

The New Language of Marketing 2.0

How to Use ANGELS to Energize Your Market

by Sandy Carter

ISBN: 0-13-714249-8

From developing the right strategies to energizing your channels of communication, this book will serve as a useful guide to the new technologies that are driving change in marketing and unlocks the secrets to new methods of communicating: Blogs, wikis, video, viral marketing, e-mail, and Web communications. Through the reach of the Internet, the marketer is not—and ought not to be—at the center of successful marketing. The customer is the center now. The Internet allows customers to opt-in or select the message that most clearly resonates with them. They choose to read an interesting blog, watch entertaining viral video, cruise Virtual Worlds, and speak through Avatars. What does this mean to us? It means that the previously separate worlds of marketing and communications are merging: Marketing 2.0 is about marketing through communication.

Listen to the author's podcast at:
ibmpressbooks.com/podcasts

Reaching The Goal

How Managers Improve a Services Business Using Goldratt's Theory of Constraints

by John Arthur Ricketts

ISBN: 0-13-233312-0

Managing services is extremely challenging, and traditional "industrial" management techniques are no longer adequate. In *Reaching The Goal*, John Arthur Ricketts presents a breakthrough management approach that embraces what makes services different: their diversity, complexity, and unique distribution methods.

Ricketts draws on Eli Goldratt's Theory of Constraints (TOC), one of this generation's most successful management methodologies... thoroughly adapting it to the needs of today's professional, scientific, and technical services businesses. He reveals how to identify the surprising constraints that limit your organization's performance, execute more effectively within those constraints, and then loosen or even eliminate them.

Listen to the author's podcast at:
ibmpressbooks.com/podcasts

Visit ibmpressbooks.com
for all product information

Related Books of Interest

The New Language of Business

Carter

ISBN: 0-13-195654-X

Executing SOA

Bieberstein, Laird, Jones, Mitra

ISBN: 0-13-235374-1

Enterprise Master Data Management

Dreibelbis, Hechler, Milman, Oberhofer, van Run, Wolfson

ISBN: 0-13-236625-8

Inescapable Data

Stakutis, Webster

ISBN: 0-13-185215-9

Irresistible! Markets, Models, and Meta-Value in Consumer Electronics

Bailey, Wenzek

ISBN: 0-13-198758-5

Can Two Rights Make a Wrong?

Moulton Reger

ISBN: 0-13-173294-3

Sign up for the monthly IBM Press newsletter at ibmpressbooks/newsletters

Praise for *Agile Career Development*

"In the 21st century, there will be an increasing competitive need for any company to operate as a globally integrated enterprise that can effectively develop and then tap the skills and capabilities of its workforce anywhere in the world. At IBM, we have worked to enable a workforce that is adaptive, flexible, and capable of responding to changes in the marketplace and the needs of our clients. *Agile Career Development* shows how focusing on career development opportunities and guidance for employees is a key factor in our business strategy and a major source of value for IBM employees. This book can be used as a guide to any organization that is seeking to find practical ways to develop the talent of its workforce."

—**J. Randall MacDonald**, Senior Vice President, IBM Human Resources

"*Agile Career Development* provides a roadmap for the development of essential capabilities and expertise at IBM. A core feature of the book is a demonstration of how IBM utilizes a structured career development process to support career growth—a blended learning approach that presents employees with options for creating meaning and purpose in their jobs and learning experience. A cornerstone of career development at IBM is the concept of accelerating the learning process by taking into consideration the personalized needs of each employee with the ultimate goal of driving business growth. This book serves as a guide to connecting learning and development to the long-term health of the business."

—**Frank Persico**, Vice President, Workforce Learning and Development, IBM Corporation

"This book highlights tried and true best practices developed at a company known the world over for active dedication to their workforce. Mary Ann, Diana, and Sheila have captured the key issues that will enhance and streamline your career development program, and subsequently increase employee engagement, retention, and productivity. I particularly like their practical, real-life understanding of the barriers to most career development programs and the manageable framework to bring career growth to life. They also teach us how to make a business case for career development—critical in creating the foundation for a sustainable program. This includes a good blend of benefits both for the individual employee and the organization as a whole. I only wish I had this book available to me years ago when I was managing a career development program!"

—**Jim Kirkpatrick**, Ph.D., author of *Implementing the Four Levels of Transferring Learning to Behavior*

"Winning companies have always recognized that career development and talent management are essential enablers to achieving business success. When organizations make a deliberate effort to invest in talent development, they are in essence creating an environment that motivates and inspires its people to raise their level of play. Employees become more engaged and committed. This book brings clarity to the business case for development and training and offers some practical and simple ways to help employees increase their value to the organization and ultimately to the marketplace."

—**Nancy J. Lewis**, Vice President and Chief Learning Officer, ITT Corporation

Agile Career Development

Lessons and Approaches from IBM

Mary Ann Bopp
Diana A. Bing
Sheila Forte-Trammell

IBM Press
Pearson plc

Upper Saddle River, NJ • Boston • Indianapolis • San Francisco
New York • Toronto • Montreal • London • Munich • Paris • Madrid
Cape Town • Sydney • Tokyo • Singapore • Mexico City

ibmpressbooks.com

IBM Press Program Managers: Steven Stansel, Ellice Uffer
Cover design: IBM Corporation

Associate Publisher: Greg Wiegand
Marketing Manager: Kourtnaye Sturgeon
Acquisitions Editor: Katherine Bull
Publicist: Heather Fox
Development Editor: Todd Brakke
Managing Editor: Kristy Hart
Designer: Alan Clements
Project Editor: Anne Goebel
Copy Editor: Language Logistics
Indexer: Lisa Stumpf
Compositor: Nonie Ratcliff
Proofreader: Williams Woods Publishing
Manufacturing Buyer: Dan Uhrig

Published by Pearson plc
Publishing as IBM Press

IBM Press offers excellent discounts on this book when ordered in quantity for bulk purchases or special sales, which may include electronic versions and/or custom covers and content particular to your business, training goals, marketing focus, and branding interests. For more information, please contact:

U. S. Corporate and Government Sales
1-800-382-3419
corpsales@pearsontechgroup.com.

For sales outside the U. S., please contact:

International Sales
international@pearsoned.com.

Library of Congress Cataloging-in-Publication Data

Bopp, Mary Ann.

Agile career development : lessons and approaches from IBM / Mary Ann Bopp, Diana A. Bing, Sheila Forte-Trammell. — 1st ed.

p. cm.

ISBN 978-0-13-715364-0

1. Career development. I. Bing, Diana A. II. Forte-Trammell, Sheila. III. International Business Machines Corporation. IV. Title.

HF5381.B635166 2009

650.14—dc22

2009023591

Pearson Education, Inc
Rights and Contracts Department
501 Boylston Street, Suite 90
Boston, MA 02116
Fax (617) 671-3447

ISBN-13: 978-0-13-715364-0
ISBN-10: 0-13-715364-3

Text printed in the United States on recycled paper at R.R. Donnelley in Crawfordsville, Indiana.

First printing August 2009

The authors would like to give special thanks to the people at IBM® that have developed the many programs mentioned in this book. Without you, this book would not have been possible as you have made IBM's career development processes and programs what they are today and will be tomorrow.

Mary Ann Bopp would like to thank the following people: My mother, Constance MacGiffert, who always inspired me to be me; my step-father, Wilfred "Bud" MacGiffert, who has inspired me through his life stories; and many other family members who are part of my life including my four brothers, Joe and John Barca and Paul and Robert MacGiffert, and their families; two stepsons, Bryan and Gary Bopp and their families; and many other extended family members and friends. Tremendous thanks to my husband, Christopher H. Bopp, who encouraged me to write this book and gave me the gift of time to dedicate to working on this project.

Diana A. Bing would like to extend special thanks to my husband Jerold Lawson and my son Tyler Bing-Lawson for their love and support. A special thanks to Dan Grandstaff and Tobie Kranitz Walters for their friendship and encouragement. Also, many thanks to my incredibly patient friends and family, all of whom are undoubtedly tired of hearing me say, "I can do it as soon as the book is done!"

Sheila Forte-Trammell would like to thank the many people who have encouraged and inspired me over the years. Foremost, to my parents whose mantra is "As you receive, so must you give." This has guided me through my life and career at IBM, and my hope is that in some small way I am able to impact others, especially the generations of IBMers behind me. I am forever grateful to my daughters Jamila and Aisha who have always told me "Go for it," and to my husband Gus Trammell who is the "wind beneath my wings." To my siblings, Carl Miller, Doreen Miller-Diagne, and Sandra Miller-Hall: I thank you for your love, your friendship, and for being my role models.

Contents

Foreword

Today's global marketplace is dynamic and extremely competitive, which puts new and different pressures on companies to remain relevant to their clients.

Twenty-first century clients expect and demand rapid response to their needs, and "good enough" service is just no longer acceptable. Solutions and services must be of the highest quality, and in order to keep current clients and attract new ones, organizations must aim to exceed client expectations.

While it is extremely important for global companies such as IBM to be attentive to the fluid needs of the marketplace, it is just as important to invest in having a portfolio of enduring skills and expertise within the company to satisfy the needs of clients regardless of where they might be located.

In fact, Thomas J. Watson, Jr. made it clear that vision, innovation, and inspiration are necessary to build an enduring company that will remain successful despite market changes and competition. In 1960 he stated, "Service has always been a hallmark of our company, and looking at the years ahead, I think that the margin between our success and failure will be measured more and more in terms of the service we provide. I am speaking not only of the service we agree to provide by contract but also of that quality of urgency expressed by people who desire to do a little more than is expected." A company must make the investment to help its people acquire the necessary skills to deliver solutions that exceed expectations. IBM has a longstanding history of developing its people, not only because it is the right thing to do, but also because of the business imperative to do so.

IBM has reinvented itself periodically, based on extensive marketplace analysis and projections. In order for IBM—or any company for that matter—to compete and win in the marketplace, it must be proactive in restructuring and redesigning the way business is conducted. As companies conduct forecasting of business trends it is important to also engage in skills, competencies, and capabilities forecasting. The development of a plan to provide an end-to-end learning process is also critical and will enable employees to build multidisciplinary skills essential to the business.

While the twenty-first century presents a new set of business challenges, it also presents opportunities that are steadily unfolding over time. Employees who are fully engaged and share in this excitement are poised to continuously learn, refresh, and enhance their skills portfolios.

As a high-performing and globally-integrated enterprise, IBM has created a culture of continuous learning in which employees are given the encouragement and appropriate tools to share knowledge with their colleagues across business units, geography and culture. In order to achieve this level of collaboration, geographic and business unit lines of demarcation must be removed, as they serve only to create barriers and impede the easy flow of information and knowledge sharing.

IBM's learning strategy articulates that "The globally-integrated enterprise will require fundamentally different approaches to production, distribution, and workforce deployment. The single most important challenge in shifting to globally-integrated enterprises, and the consideration driving most business decisions today, will be securing a supply of high-value skills across the world. Our people are a critical factor to achieving long-term profitable growth. Supporting our learning strategy is an investment in the future of IBM. The learning function's role is to help our company learn, adopt, adapt and grow." IBM has invested time and dollars in identifying disparate, disjointed, redundant and low-value processes across the globe. The goal of this investment is to simplify, consolidate, and reuse best practices in a purposeful manner across the globe. This approach also includes the way we deliver learning and train employees to enhance current skills and acquire new ones, enabling the company to focus on the demands of the marketplace by providing the right skills in the right place at the right time. This is why it is important that employees be fully engaged to build their knowledge base and skills. Furthermore, as employees grow capabilities over time, they should be held accountable for passing on this knowledge to anyone, anywhere in the business. As individual capabilities are built, organizational capabilities are strengthened. Once this occurs, the organization becomes adaptable to changes created by the marketplace.

An adaptive workforce is characterized by the skills and expertise levels that exist within the organization. Because of this, the enterprise is always in a mode of readiness to respond swiftly to the needs of its global clients. A by-product of a globally-integrated enterprise is that the leaders of the organization know who has the skills and where they exist, and they are in a position to unleash these skills to address global marketplace problems or to deliver solutions and services at a moment's notice.

Agile Career Development: Lessons and Approaches from IBM is a timely book that is pertinent to any organization because it addresses a variety of topics that many companies are grappling with today. The core elements of the book illustrate in a practical manner the remaking of IBM's career development processes to attract, retain, and engage employees through learning and development supported by a common, enterprise-wide career framework. The authors show how IBM developed a one-stop approach to career development tools and resources and in the process empower employees to use these resources to assess their skills gaps and develop learning plans to close the gaps.

Overall, IBM's investment in career development is about workforce effectiveness and optimization, where expertise is a cornerstone that drives employee performance as well as organization performance. As IBM develops its Human Capital capabilities, it stands to reap dividends by providing ever-increasing shareholder value and success in the marketplace.

—**Ted Hoff**, Vice President, IBM Center for Learning and Development

Acknowledgments

This book represents the expertise and passion of a tremendous global team that has worked tirelessly in recent years to innovate, create, and execute world-class career development resources for all IBM employees. Without you, we would not have a story to tell.

The authors would like to thank the following reviewers for their time, expertise, and gracious critiques in helping to shape our work:

Sharon Arad, Ph.D.
Anne Lake
Lindsay-Rae McIntyre
Renae Murphy
Audrey Murrell, Ph.D.
Reza Sisakhti, Ph.D.
Charlotte Wooten

Special thanks to Tobie Kranitz Walters, who provided the authors tremendous insight and perspectives with an external view; to Brenda Thompson and Olivia Robinson for helping to coordinate meetings with the author team; to Terris Richardson for her research support; to Dr. Ronald Shapiro for analysis of job/role responsibility; to Michael Cannon, Phee Vania, and the New Employee Experience team for input on the Your IBM+ program; to Matthew Valencius for input on the Global Sales School program; to Frank Persico, who has been instrumental in helping us drive many of the new career development changes cited in the book; and, last but not least, to the IBM Press team.

Many thanks to Ted Hoff for writing the Foreword.

The authors would also like to thank the Pearson Education team, Katherine Bull, Acquisitions Editor, and Todd Brakke, Development Editor, for their knowledge and support throughout the entire writing experience. Their professionalism provided the guiding light for us to achieve our best.

About the Authors

Mary Ann Bopp is Manager of Career Development for the IBM Center for Learning and Development. She leads global career development initiatives for all IBM employees. Many of these programs have won external awards or citations from the Society of Human Resource Management (SHRM), the American Society of Training & Development (ASTD), and Brandon Hall Research. She is also the recipient of various internal IBM awards in recognition of her work achievements. She has over 21 years of career development program management experience and ten years of management accounting experience. She is a volunteer member of the Accounting Advisory Committee for Dutchess Community College in Poughkeepsie, NY, providing counsel to the committee for accounting skill needs of business students.

Diana A. Bing recently retired from IBM. Her last position at IBM was Corporate Director, Enterprise Learning. In that position, she designed and introduced career, professional, and technical development for IBM's worldwide employee population. Programs included new employee orientation, career framework and progression, competence development, mentoring, job rotation and exploration, skills initiatives, and technical development. Her programs and initiatives won numerous awards from prestigious organizations such as ASTD, Brandon Hall, and SHRM. Over the years she has served on many community organizations, as well as non-profit, educational and global innovation initiatives and boards. She is an executive professional coach and is a speaker on career, multicultural, and women's issues. Diana is coauthor of *Intelligent Mentoring: How IBM Creates Value through People, Knowledge, and Relationships.*

Sheila Forte-Trammell is a Learning Consultant for the IBM Center for Learning and Development and has extensive knowledge and experience in a variety of Human Resources disciplines. She has a record of designing global programs with the goal to develop, retain, and engage employees. Through these initiatives, employees are able to feel welcomed and valued in the IBM workplace. As a result of her many contributions, Sheila has received several IBM awards as well as national recognition. Sheila is also a keynote speaker and seminar presenter at several national conferences and considers herself a servant of the community. She is coauthor of *Intelligent Mentoring: How IBM Creates Value through People, Knowledge, and Relationships.*

Chapter 1 Contents

I

Having the Right Skills in the Right Place at the Right Time

"There are some who might look upon the schoolhouse as additional expense, but we who have had experience in this business know it is a good investment. It is a source of extra profit, because through intelligent use of it we are going to educate people and make money out of our business."

–Thomas J. Watson, 1933

"Learning is not compulsory but neither is survival."

–W. Edwards Deming

Career Development? Who Cares? You Should.

Over the past several years, the flurry of advances in technology, fueled by the globalization of work, the integration of global financial markets and economies, as well as the economic downturn, provide a platform for both opportunities and challenges that have not been experienced in the past. At the same time, the notion of career development is changing as companies continue to require a diverse, resilient, and flexible workforce that is highly skilled as well as adaptable to shifts in market demands.

Career development was once like a sleepy little town in the business world—predictable and unchanging, where everyone knew what to expect. If someone wanted to advance toward a particular position, the path to get there was clear. You entered a company; you knew where you were starting and what needed to be done to progress to the next level. It was predictable, expected, and presumptive.

Then in the last decade, everything began to change. Along with the advent of globalization has come an increased level of complexity in managing business, and a current deteriorating economic situation has only exacerbated the situation. A company in today's environment must have the agility to quickly and effectively change the way decisions are made within its organizational structure and systems. Career development is one of the areas where agility is key. The most progressive and successful businesses have come to realize that career development is not just a nice-to-have adjunct program in Human Resources (HR). Rather, having an agile, flexible career development process in place has become a major aspect of business strategy because having the right people in the right jobs at the right time is one of the best ways to assure on-going client satisfaction.

According to Brook Manville, businesses began to realize that "...a company's skills, knowledge and people, and how they are managed, developed and deployed, is the heart of value creation."[1]

IBM® has always valued learning and career development but has come to realize that traditional approaches to it were no longer adequate. Working for a company one's entire career, advancing predictably through the ranks, was no longer the norm, as was noted in an IBM White Paper:

> We knew that successfully growing the business hinged on our ability to put the full depth and breadth of our most significant

> resource—the global workforce—to work for clients efficiently and effectively. If we did this right, we would distinguish ourselves as a global innovator in quickly matching the best skilled employees with business opportunities.[2]

Education and learning have always been important at IBM, leading to a strong legacy in ensuring that employees were positioned to have the future skills and expertise needed to meet client requirements. An important part of this career development philosophy was the opportunity for employees to have a voice in their own personal career aspirations. Early career development processes and programs at IBM were rather simplistic compared to the needs of today's complex workplace. At least on an annual basis, the manager and employee determined what skills might be required to meet business goals, discussed aspirations, and put a learning plan in place to move the employee—as well as the business—toward a mutually-acceptable objective. While many managers and employees followed this approach, which worked quite well, the complexity of business grew, and globalization became a critical business driver. As this occurred, an enterprise-wide solution for staffing and resource development became critical. Although more focused career development planning went on in specific IBM departments, no enterprise-wide solution and deployment existed. In the early 2000s, however, the company began re-engineering the way it cultivated and deployed its talented workforce, both in terms of matching available people to existing work opportunities and developing them for new assignments.

It was important for IBM to position itself to meet the ever-changing needs of its global client base. Given the company's long-term history of rebranding and redefining itself based on the changing needs of the times, once IBM redefined itself to meet those needs, it was inevitable that the organization had to rethink career development. In the mid-2000s, IBM invested in developing a strategic set of processes, policies, procedures, and the integration of separate applications.[3] At about the same time, IBM identified the need for a single career framework that outlined the capabilities IBM employees need to provide client value and subsequently provided meaningful career paths for employees. IBM later went on to develop this common career framework and at the time of this writing, IBM is in the process of deploying the framework to the IBM population.

These efforts will help effectively address fluctuating market needs, continual competitive challenges, and new opportunities. It also enables IBM to begin implementing a single integrated, worldwide approach to hiring, developing, deploying and managing its workforce. It provides a full view of employee skills and expertise and allows individual IBMers much greater clarity and visibility about career development. Throughout this book, we explore these many facets of IBM's approach to career development.

Why Career Development Is Paramount to a Company's Strategy

Just as a manufacturing company must build an effective supply chain to ensure that it has all the necessary parts on hand to fabricate its products, other types of companies also need to make sure that they have people with the right skills, talent, knowledge, and expertise to carry out the business functions that deliver the value for which their clients are looking.

In a competitive business environment, the edge goes to the company that has the products and services that its clients require. But developing and delivering those products and services is a function of people and teams who create the ideas and engineer the products. They must also solve the manufacturing or delivery problems while building relationships with clients in order to provide the most effective outcomes. This has to be a deliberate and well-orchestrated process with many steps. Each step requires knowledge and expertise delivered by a trained human being.

The company's business strategy will determine the expertise and performance requirements needed to fulfill each business function. In other words, the business priorities determine the human capital requirements, including the learning and career development strategies. To get the desired business results, the organization must identify the needed knowledge and skills, determine expertise levels and gaps, and create and implement a career development strategy for achieving the required levels of capabilities needed. Career development thus becomes the essential driver of bottom-line results. In fact, as D.M. Gayeski noted in 2005, "The ability of organizations to specify goals and then to engineer the desired performance by training, sharing knowledge and providing feedback is one of the most important factors to success."[4]

No matter the size of a company, career development is vital to its success and ability to grow. Even the smallest business must engage in career development to determine what skills and abilities are needed to serve its clients. Employees who have benefited from meaningful development plans are more technically proficient, motivated, and focused on client needs. They find meaning in their work, and this motivation enables them to discover what interests them and helps them work toward greater performance.

Career development processes can work as a change agent[5] to help link individual goals to business goals and objectives so that employees gain long-term capabilities that both advance their own careers and are also supportive of the company's strategic plans. The organization saves money by having people focus on things that are important to the business, and the employee is assured that the time and effort put into training and development will result in career advancement because it has been tied into what the company values.

For career development to be used as a change agent, companies need to be sure that employees have opportunities to acquire and apply new skills that focus not just on their current jobs and their next jobs, but also on the longer term. It behooves companies to encourage their employees to develop a broad and diverse portfolio of capabilities to offer in a variety of roles. This implies that both managers and employees must be of the mindset that development means employees are either moving horizontally and gaining new experiences or moving up the ladder—or getting ready to do so.

Change, Complexity, and Globalization

With the rapid changes taking place in technology, including the globalization of economies and the integration of markets, not only must skills be learned, but they also must be learned quickly and continuously. In addition, the economic downturn could potentially change client needs in the future. Thought leaders such as Thomas Friedman have identified at least three forces that are driving organizations to think more strategically about how to create high-performance workplaces, thus affecting career development. They are

- The exponential pace of change
- The intensifying complexity of the world
- Globalization of business and work[6]

Technology is changing with breathtaking speed, affecting both the workforce itself, as well as the process of career management. This exponential pace of change underscores the importance of having a workforce that can readily adapt to and embrace any and all changes. Employees who are most valuable to the company are those who can not only pick up new knowledge quickly and efficiently, but also those who can accept the fact that today's essential skills may well be obsolete by tomorrow and that a skill that will be essential tomorrow does not even exist today.

For example, in the software field, new skills requirements arise daily in terms of Internet communication, security, and development. It is imperative that companies keep abreast of new software developments so that they are able to offer employees training in the latest skills. And employees must not be content to rest on their laurels, but always be ready to learn something new. The company that provides career development for people to learn and/or retrain in a newly developing software technology might win both in attracting and keeping valuable employees and by being able to move quickly into a new market.

Increasingly, complexity—as well as the rapid pace of change—requires more frequent and continuous updating of knowledge, skills, and learning. Collaborating, mentoring, and providing the tools for knowledge sharing are more important than ever.

This complexity is also manifested in the way that the global economy has changed with "the inexorable integration of markets, nation-states, and technologies to a degree never witnessed before—in a way that is enabling individuals, corporations, and nation-states to reach around the world farther, faster, deeper, and cheaper than ever before..."[7] Technological advances over the past decade or so have made the marketplace exponentially more competitive, and the competition is no longer local; it is global. The talent pool is no longer local; it is global. Flatter, more integrated global teams provide true competitive advantage. Technology has an impact on everything. Demographic shifts constantly change the marketplace, affecting everything from labor sourcing to channel distribution. When a company thinks of competition, it must think in terms of marketplace *and* talent.

Anything that a company can do to outpace the competition is vitally important to that organization's on-going survival. Naturally, companies must have the best products and/or services, competitive pricing, a strong presence in the marketplace, and widespread, efficient distribution. Equally important is having an effective career development system in place so that the company's product or service is delivered by employees who are continuously trained with the latest knowledge and are enthusiastic about their jobs.

However, creating an adaptable workforce is not an easy thing to do, and it requires more than a series of HR programs. It starts at the top with key leaders. These leaders must develop and communicate a vision while providing structure and guidance, and ultimately delivering business results. As was determined from the study, "Unlocking the DNA of the Adaptable Workforce," done by IBM Global Business Services, "having an adaptable workforce requires that the company be able to identify experts and foster an environment where knowledge and experience travel beyond traditional organizational boundaries. It calls for a talent model that can help companies recruit, develop, and retain valued segments of the employee population. It depends on an underlying backbone of data and information about the current and projected state of workforce performance and the ability to apply that information to develop strategic insights and recommendations. The adaptable workforce is a precursor for future organizational success."[8]

Career Development Impacts the Bottom Line

Having people with the right expertise aligned with the needs of the organization is necessary for business effectiveness. Yet in a 2007 IBM-conducted study of 400 organizations across many industries,[9] more than half of the study participants surveyed indicated that the inability to rapidly develop skills was a primary workforce challenge, and more than one-third stated their employees' skills were not aligned with their current organizational priorities; specifically, skill development was not keeping pace with organizational change and priorities.

When participating organizations were asked what they saw as the primary workforce-related issues facing their organizations, almost all of the challenges cited were closely related to career development concerns which had a strong correlation to the bottom line.[10]

Research has been conducted that shows a strong correlation between employee engagement and company performance. Towers Perrin, in their 2007 Global Workforce Study,[11] looked at 50 global companies over a one-year period, correlating their employee engagement levels with financial results. The companies with high employee engagement enjoyed a 19% increase in operating income and nearly 28% growth in earnings per share (EPS), while those with low levels of engagement lost more than 32% in operating income and over 11% in EPS.[12]

In addition, the percentage of employees who believe they can have an impact on a range of business metrics increases along with their level of engagement.[13]

More engaged employees are also more likely to stay with their companies. However, as the Towers Perrin study also notes, 40% of employees are "passive job seekers," open to other opportunities, although not actively looking. What's worse is that half of the disengaged workers have no plans to leave or are not looking for other jobs. This means employers could lose the workers they would most like to keep, while keeping the ones who are not really adding to the company's success.

Thus, employers cannot afford to be complacent about their engaged employees, given that engagement in and of itself does not ensure retention. One of the ways to retain employees is by having a competitive salary and benefits package but along with that, offering employees a top-notch career development plan can help keep the engaged in place.

The study confirms the importance of the organization itself creating the conditions that drive engagement. Key factors are the actions and behavior of senior management, the organization's image and reputation, and the learning and development opportunities the organization provides.[14]

Engagement is about motivating employees to go the extra mile in the workplace. It is about encouraging employees to have a passion for their work and identifying the organization as more than a place to earn money. A *Harvard Business Review* article explained that "employees are motivated by jobs that challenge them and enable them to grow and learn, and they are demoralized by those that seem to be monotonous or to lead to a dead end."[15]

In 2006, The Conference Board published "Employee Engagement, A Review of Current Research and Its Implications." According to this report, 12 major studies on employee engagement had been published over the prior four years by top research firms such as Gallup, Towers Perrin, Blessing White, the Corporate Leadership Council, and others. The Conference Board defines employee engagement as "a heightened emotional connection that an employee feels for his or her organization, that influences him or her to exert greater discretionary effort to his or her work."

The studies identified eight key drivers, half of which are related to career development. These key drivers are as follows:

- **Trust and integrity**—How well do managers communicate and "walk the talk?"
- **Nature of the job**—Is it mentally stimulating day-to-day?
- **Line of sight between employee performance and company performance**—Do employees understand how their work contributes to the company's performance?
- **Career growth opportunities**—Are there future opportunities for growth?
- **Pride in the company**—How much self-esteem do employees feel by being associated with their company?
- **Coworkers/team members**—Do they significantly influence an employee's level of engagement?
- **Employee development**—Is the company making an effort to develop the employees' skills?
- **Relationship with management**—Do employees value the relationship with their managers?[16]

Another study, The *SHRM 2006 Job Satisfaction Survey Report*,[17] clearly showed that learning/career development is an important factor of workplace satisfaction. The list of "very important" aspects of employee job satisfaction within career development consists of 1) the opportunities to use skills/abilities; 2) career development opportunities; 3) career advancement opportunities; and 4) the importance of the organization's commitment to professional development.

As a Mercer consulting study indicated, "organizations that are committed to actively managing careers for both business' and the individual's benefit will win the race to attract, engage, and retain their workforces. They have realized that, in addition to compensation and benefits, employees consider career-related rewards, including training and development, lateral moves, stretch assignments, and career incentive—a significant and highly motivating component of total rewards. These are the organizations with higher performance, employee engagement, and retention—the ones that will be best positioned to deliver career outcomes and improved business results."[18]

Models for Career Development

If a conductor wants to form an orchestra that will make beautiful music, he must first determine the mix of stringed instruments, woodwinds, brass, and percussion that he wants. He will then seek to fill the available spots with the best musicians he can find and retain in each instrumental category. The orchestra's musical repertoire and audience will be largely determined by the balance and skill level of the musicians the conductor attracts. Similarly, businesses decide on what mix of knowledge and skill they need to make the particular "music" that is their product and service mix. Much of their success depends on how much talent they are able to attract and retain.

Unlike orchestras that tend to use many of the same instruments and music that have been around for a couple hundred years, businesses face the challenge that their "violins" might be outdated tomorrow, and the "woodwinds" of today could be replaced by totally different technology that does not even exist today. Having people with the right talents and expertise is a complex undertaking that focuses not only on current needs but also on an uncertain future based on factors such as: changing technology, anticipated client needs, market trends, economic impacts, and shifting population trends.

In every business, the key question for creating a career development strategy is what skills and knowledge are needed in order to compete, carry out business strategies, and provide maximum (or on-going) value to clients? This approach to career development strategy is depicted in Figure 1.1.

It would be extremely shortsighted of a company to base its strategy solely on the product or service it wanted to provide without understanding what the marketplace is looking for. A company enhances its strategy by taking into account external factors—such as economic conditions, government regulations, and the flattening effect of globalization—and determining the impact that these opportunities and threats will have on client requirements. After these factors are determined, they will then influence the company's business strategy. This, in turn, has an impact on the company's talent requirements, resultant talent strategy, and ultimately its career development and learning offerings. In this manner, the company is assured that the knowledge its employees are gaining will

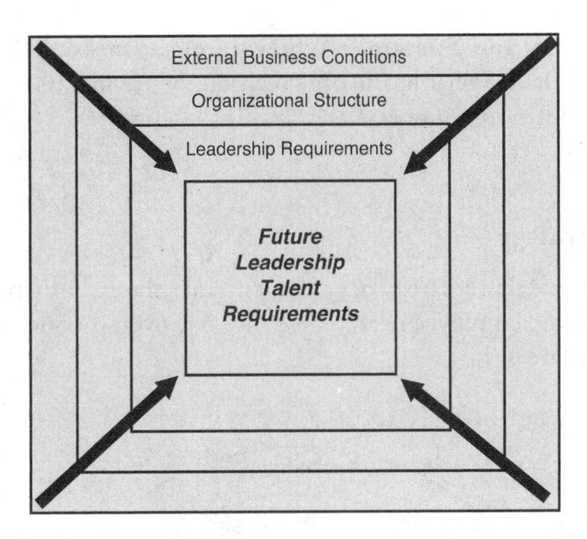

Figure 1.1 Creating a career development strategy.[19]

have the greatest possible positive impact on their ability to address client issues in the marketplace, making the company the provider of choice.

Career development is an integral component of the overall talent management strategy, not a stand-alone component. There are six dimensions of a talent management strategy:

1. **Develop Strategy**—Establishing the optimal long-term strategy for attracting, developing, connecting, and deploying the workforce
2. **Attract and Retain**—Sourcing, recruiting, and holding onto those who have the appropriate expertise, according to business needs
3. **Motivate and Develop**—Verifying that people's capabilities are understood and developed to match business requirement, while also meeting people's needs for motivation, development, and job satisfaction
4. **Deploy and Manage**—Providing effective resource deployment, scheduling, and work management that matches skills and experience with organizational needs
5. **Connect and Enable**—Identifying individuals with relevant skills, collaborating and sharing knowledge, and working effectively in virtual settings

6. **Transform and Sustain**—Achieving clear, measurable, and sustainable change within the organization, while maintaining the day to day continuity of operations[20]

Develop Strategy

IBM's approach to career development integrates both the business strategy and the employee perspective into one overall understanding, as shown in Figure 1.2.

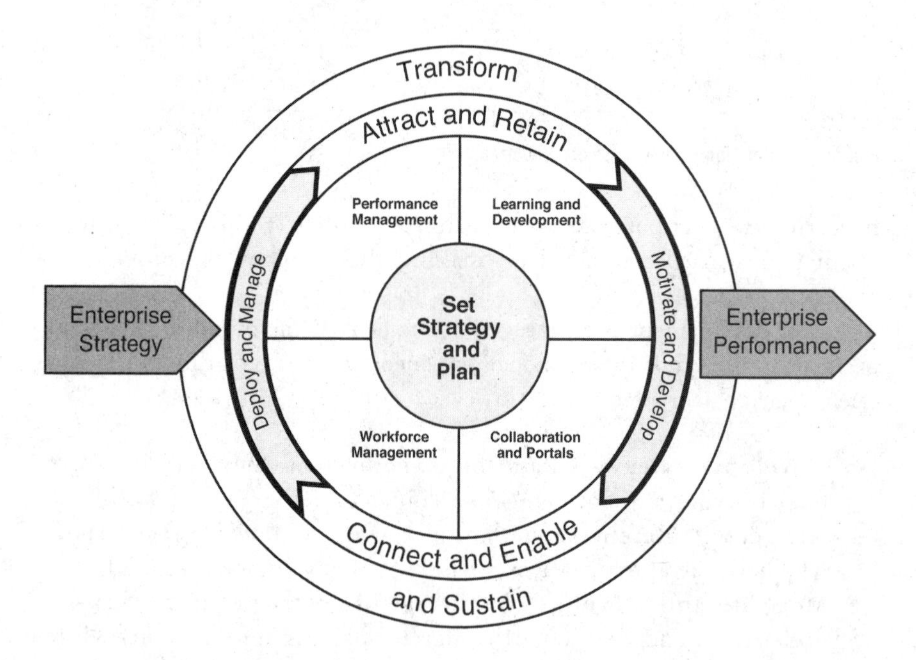

Figure 1.2 The career development process: business and employee perspective.

Incorporating the career model into the overall workforce talent management strategy and plan demonstrates clear linkages to business and financial goals. It also embeds career messaging into strategic corporate communications. As IBM senior executive Ginni Rometty said in a 2007 Quarterly Executive Call, "There is no sustainable business model...without a sustainable people model."

Attract and Retain Talent

To attract and retain talent, a company needs to offer their employees compelling career paths and exciting opportunities. Company image and reputation as a good place to work are very important factors in attracting top talent. The way to retain this talent is by offering clear and concise career advancement guidance, additional development opportunities, rotational assignments, mentoring, and access to professional communities. The Towers Perrin study referenced earlier noted that "One of the top drivers of attraction, retention and engagement is career advancement, potential career tracks, and skill/capability development opportunities."[21]

In Chapter 2, "Enabling Career Advancement," and Chapter 4, "Selecting the Best Talent and Developing New Employees," we talk about how IBM formalized its process for attracting, developing, and retaining its skilled workforce by developing a common language for defining job roles, describing advancement opportunities, and creating a system whereby employees could match their interests to the needs of the company.

Motivate and Develop

Employees must clearly understand what they need to do to reach the next step. They need to have a framework by which to align expertise development with overall career progression. Given this structure, future leaders who possess the required level of skills and capabilities are thus able to succeed in multiple roles. In a 2007 article, *Fast Company* noted that "the mantra of the emerging workforce is 'Develop me or I'm history.' They're building their portfolios and beefing up their resumes. It may seem counterintuitive, but helping them grow will help you keep them."[22]

The career development portion of IBM's workforce strategy, which outlines the particular skills employees need to help the company accomplish its goals, is instrumental in determining where to invest in employee training in order to meet client needs. In Chapter 3, "Defining the Career Development Process," we show how the career development process provides employees a meaningful and motivating way to advance in their careers.

Deploy and Manage

Encouraging employees to move within or across departments helps them gain experience and develop in new ways. The currency of skills supports deployment and workforce optimization. They also help business leaders and HR identify both gaps and gluts in skills and capabilities, thereby enhancing the value of workforce analytics to the business and influencing sourcing strategies. McKinsey research noted that organizations "should also make bold moves to break down internal silos by moving talent around (e.g., through rotations and international assignments).[23]

Several years ago, IBM piloted a formal experiential learning program (introduced in Chapter 3 and further explored in Chapter 8, "Linking Collaborative Learning Activities to Development Plans") that helps employees learn through experienced-based stretch assignments, cross-unit projects, job rotations, and more. The program was extremely successful and has now been expanded throughout the company.

Connect and Enable

An effective working and learning environment gives employees the tools and resources they need and helps them connect with others. The goal is to establish enterprise-wide professional communities to support employee development, professional leadership and knowledge sharing, and to connect employees with each other for mentoring and social networking. Web-enabled career and development resources and tools should be made available for on-demand career planning and development. A Towers Perrin study in 2007 found that, relative to industry benchmarks, companies with higher levels of employee engagement tend to outperform those with lower employee engagement on key financial measures.[24]

At IBM, a number of communities have been established to help employees collaborate with each other, learn, and grow. As is further discussed in Chapter 6, "Building Employee and Organizational Capability," these communities include both formal and informal ones, supported by subject matter experts and bound by the members' commitment to giving back to the community as well as benefiting from it.

Transform and Sustain

The accelerating forces of change require that businesses and employees be continually transformed from the known and familiar to the unknown and the uncertain. This transformation can be exciting at times, but it can also be extremely challenging and even disorienting. Such transformation requires that the business continually ask how it can have the right people with the right skills now and tomorrow and the year after, even though no one can foresee what kinds of opportunities or challenges the next year will bring. The transformation for employees requires a degree of flexibility and adaptability they may never have known before.

In the midst of this invigorating and disorienting transformation, the business must also create ways to maintain its core values and sustain itself as an organization. It must provide a sense of "orientation and knowing" for employees so they can tolerate and even thrive in the midst of all the change and uncertainty. We believe that career development can and must play a key role in sustaining the organization with its core values and sense of mission, as well as provide a kind of "ever-changing stability" for employees. Like a gyroscope that keeps a rocket from spinning out of control even as it speeds on its way, career development can be a sustaining and balancing force for both the business and its employees. Those businesses and their employees that have the ability to adapt and change as the market indicators require will have a resiliency that will drive growth and profitability.

The IBM Approach: Essential Components of Career Development

At IBM, managing and growing global talent includes the following two broad areas:

- Skill anticipation and building to meet current and emerging marketplace needs
- Rapid deployment in terms of filling jobs and staffing projects so that the workforce can solve client problems efficiently and effectively

The overall objective is to be sure that the right person with the right skills is on the right job, quickly and cost-effectively. When this happens, the company profits from enhanced competitiveness, based on its ability to hire, manage, and deploy a professional workforce on a worldwide basis. Managers are more helpful to their employees and more collaborative on employee career development, while the employees receive much greater clarity, visibility, and ultimately opportunities for career development.[25]

Career development needs to be a working component of the overall talent management strategy and plan. It should be integrated with other plan components and should demonstrate clear linkages to business and financial goals. By improving workforce effectiveness, the business then enables enterprise innovation and performance.

Responsive and Resilient Workforce

There can be no doubt that winning in competitive and quickly shifting global markets requires organizations to be responsive. The global economy is transforming into an integrated market, full of opportunity, competition, and constant change.

It has come to light that the best career development practices focus on several critical components: first and foremost, developing an adaptable workforce; revealing leadership gaps; cracking the code for talent; and driving growth through workforce analysis. There are several key elements required to put these practices in place:

- Ensuring that the talent strategy is determined by the business and market strategy
- Rapidly developing skills to address current/future business needs
- Developing leadership capability
- Aligning with current organizational priorities
- Collaborating on/sharing knowledge across the organization
- Attracting qualified candidates
- Building an engaged/motivated workforce
- Redeploying/realigning resources against new opportunities
- Retaining key employees

Linking Performance Management to Career Development

According to the U.S. Office of Personnel Management (OPM), performance management is the systematic process by which a business involves its employees, as individuals and members of a group, in improving organizational effectiveness in the accomplishment of company mission and goals. Performance management helps organizations achieve their strategic goals. Employee performance management includes:

- Planning work and setting expectations
- Continually monitoring performance
- Developing the capacity to perform
- Periodically rating performance in a summary fashion
- Rewarding good performance[26]

Managers play a key role in providing feedback of job performance, identifying skill needs, and facilitating access to development opportunities.

Learning and Development

As the lifespan of relevant skills continues to shrink, we must focus on blending classroom training with electronic learning tools. At the same time, formal instruction must be combined with informal learning opportunities, such as mentoring, peer learning, and access to user-generated content.

Focused on marketplace driving forces and client requirements, four main elements are critical:

- **Expertise-based learning**—Learning that is focused on specific expertise requirements
- **Work-based learning**—Learning and development that is integrated in the work being done
- **Performance-based learning**—Continuous feedback integrated into the learning
- **Worldwide Integrated solutions**—Shared critical content and methods while inclusive of unique geography requirements

The kind of learning IBM envisions for the future is fundamentally focused on colleagues teaching colleagues—working together to solve problems together across geographies, boundaries, time zones, and even companies.

In the past, employees who wanted to learn beyond their own company had to attend conferences or register for academic courses. Today, employees can join social networks of similar-minded people who organize themselves around subjects they care about. And these networks are not only within the company itself, but also linked to networks of people across the industries or clients the company serves.

Collaboration and Innovation

There are three major capabilities that influence the workforce's ability to adapt to change. The first is that companies need to be able to predict their future skills requirements. Second, local experts must be located and identified. And third, there must be a way for employees to collaborate across geographies, time zones, and department "silos."[27]

IBM has clearly recognized the need for knowledge transfer programs to drive innovation, with a focus on experiential learning and engagement of experts to share the "art" of their practice, as witnessed by the IBM initiatives outlined here:

- **Apprentice programs** pair experts with groups of learners to undertake problem-solving for critical activities. A key point is the integration with both their job responsibilities and their learning plans.
- **Collaboration programs** allow employees to collaborate with experts. Social networking tools provide employees with the global capacity to collaborate, allowing community and team collaboration in virtual spaces. Mentoring and coaching are used here in large part to ensure the transfer of knowledge.
- **Communities of practice** enable knowledge sharing. This is important as work occurs all over the world and employees need to have accessibility to those with the knowledge and expertise. Experts lead various communities in the transfer of knowledge and the building and capturing of best practices.
- **Learning portals** are integrated learning management systems that offer employees connections to experts, mentors and coaches, as well as links to community building and social networks. The portals promote best practices as well as skill-building, career planning, and management.

Summary

Career development is paramount to a company's business strategy and is essential to ensuring that the company will have the people with the needed skills to meet client needs in a rapidly changing global world. Career development is also a key factor in attracting, retaining, and engaging employees for increased productivity and satisfaction. To keep the best and brightest employees, career development must continually adapt to the dynamic global marketplace and to workforce needs. Companies that do this will be the ones that thrive in the coming decades. This is both the challenge and the promise of career development. In Chapter 2, we provide an overview of IBM's view of managing expertise, which is based on development of three components: competencies, which are proven key indicators of success for high-performing employees; skills in both current and hoped-for future roles; and capabilities that employees grow over time as they increase their skills and competencies and get different experiences in their current and future job roles. These components provide employees with clear guidance in how to progress in their careers, offer clients best-in-class support, and contribute to IBM's image as a market leader.

The remainder of this book is dedicated to describing an approach to career development as practiced by IBM. Chapter 3 discusses how managing expertise is supported by the various steps in the career development process used at IBM. Chapter 4 discusses ways to attract and acclimate new employees by leveraging competencies as a basis for identifying promising prospects and providing a robust orientation program over the employee's first year. In Chapter 5, "Assessing Levels of Expertise and Taking Action to Drive Business Success," readers learn to assess levels of expertise, identify needs, and examine learning activities. Growing capabilities as part of career advancement will be discussed in Chapter 6, and in Chapter 7, "Creating Meaningful Development Plans," we will talk about the creation of meaningful development plans as a mechanism for employees to take ownership of their careers. Chapter 8 shows how to supplement development plans with nontraditional forms of learning, such as mentoring and experiential, on-the-job opportunities. Finally, Chapter 9, "Measuring Success," lays out how IBM uses a robust measurement strategy to track the impact of career development and identifies critical success factors and lessons learned.

Endnotes

[1]Manville, Brook. "Organizing Enterprise-Wide E-Learning and Human Capital Management," *Chief Learning Officer*, April, 2003.

[2]IBM. "IBM is committed to employee development," IBM's Workforce Management Initiative (WMI) White Paper, 2008, p. 4.

[3]Ibid, p. 2.

[4]Gayeski, D.M. *Managing Learning and Communications Systems as Business Assets*, Pearson/Prentice Hall: Upper Saddle River, NJ, 2005.

[5]Simonson, Peggy. *Promoting a Development Culture in Your Organization: Using Career Development as a Change Agent*, Davies-Black Publishing: Washington, D.C., 1997.

[6]Friedman, Thomas L. *The World Is Flat: A Brief History of the Twenty-first Century*. New York: Farrar, Straus & Giroux, 2005.

[7]Friedman, Thomas L. *The Lexus and the Olive Tree: Understanding Globalization*. New York: Anchor Books, 2000, p. 9.

[8]IBM Global Business Services, "Unlocking the DNA of the Adaptable Workforce," The Global Human Capital Study 2008, p. 5.

[9]Ibid.

[10]Ibid.

[11]Towers Perrin Global Workforce Study 2007, "Closing the Engagement Gap: A Road Map for Driving Superior Business Performance", p.5.

[12]Ibid.

[13]Ibid, p. 6.

[14]Ibid, p. 8.

[15]Nohria, Nitin, et al., "Employee Motivation: A Powerful New Model," *Harvard Business Review*, July–August 2008, p. 81.

[16]Gibbons, John. "Employee Engagement, A Review of Current Research and Its Implications," The Conference Board, November 2006.

[17]Esen, E. SHRM 2006 Job Satisfaction Survey Report. Society for Human Resource Management, Alexandria, VA: June 2006.

[18]Mercer Human Resource Consulting, *The Career Joint Venture*. New York, 2005, p. 4.

[19]Op. cit., The Global Human Capital Study 2008, p. 5.

[20]IBM Global Business Services, "Integrated Talent Management." IBM Institute for Business Value, 2008, p. 3

[21]Towers Perrin, op. cit., p. 16.

[22]Jordan-Evans, Sharon, and Kaye, Beverly. "The Top 10 Trends for Career Development and Employee Engagement." *Fast Company*, December 2007. www.fastcompany.com/fastforward/forward-talent.html.

[23]Guthridge, Matthew, et al., "The People Problem in Talent Management." *McKinsey Quarterly*, 2006, 2:8.

[24]Op. cit., Towers Perrin Global Workforce Study.

[25]Op. cit., WMI 2008 White Paper, p. 7.

[26]U.S. Office of Personnel Management, *A Handbook for Measuring Employee Performance*, 2002, p. 5.

[27]Op. cit., The Global Human Capital Study 2008, p. 2.

Chapter 2 Contents

2

Enabling Career Advancement

Why Employees Leave...and the Connection to Career Progression

The case for career development and its contributions to improving employee engagement is now quite clear. In an online survey conducted in October 2007 by ASTD (American Society of Training & Development) in conjunction with Dale Carnegie and Associates and the Institute for Corporate Productivity (i4cp), over 750 learning, HR, and business executives and other leaders provided insights on their organizations' practices related to engagement among their workers. According to the survey, "The respondents agreed that learning plays a key role in shaping engagement, and they ranked learning activities high among the processes they now use—or should use—to engage their employees.... Respondents reported on the impact of the learning function on employee engagement when asked about the factors that influenced engagement in their organizations. Quality of workplace learning opportunities ranked first among respondents from all organizations.

Learning through stretch assignments and frequency and breadth of learning opportunities also were highly rated factors influencing engagement."[1]

It is striking that there is still an imbalance between what management thinks satisfies employees—and therefore actions organizations take to create a working environment—and what employees actually want. One might be quick to jump to the conclusion that money is the prime motivator for employee satisfaction. After all, cash is king, right? In fact, in the late 1990s, the Society for Human Resources Management (SHRM) polled its members to better understand retention factors. Survey results showed that 89% of respondents said the biggest threat to retention was "higher salaries offered by other organizations."[2] But if this is explored further, there is evidence that disputes this belief, even from writings from as early as the 1940s and 50s that sought to analyze and understand human motivation.

If we explore some of the early work of both Abraham Maslow and Frederick Herzberg, both professors of psychology, their theories of motivation provide insight into employee behavior. In 1954, Abraham Maslow published a volume of articles and papers under the title *Motivation and Personality.* His research and work established a hierarchy based on basic human needs and how this hierarchy would contribute to our understanding of motivation. He discussed these basic needs and their relationship to one another in what became known as Maslow's "hierarchy of needs."[3]

In Maslow's theory, human needs are arranged in a hierarchy of importance. Needs emerge only when higher priority needs have been satisfied. By the same token, satisfied needs no longer influence behavior. This point seems worth stressing to managers and administrators, who often mistakenly assume that money and other tangible incentives are the only cures for morale and productivity problems. It may be, however, that the need to participate, to be recognized, to be creative, and to experience a sense of worth are better motivators in an affluent society, where many have already achieved an acceptable measure of freedom from hunger and threats to security and personal safety and are now driven by higher-order psychological needs.[4]

Maslow's theory is often depicted as a triangle, where the basic needs appear on the bottom of the triangle and require fulfillment before the next need is met. Figure 2.1[5] reflects this hierarchy of needs. If this theory is applied to the workplace, the figure shows how management could provide a working environment that satisfies from the very basic needs to self-actualization. It could be argued that fulfilling self-actualization needs comes from within the person, whether that is by seeking employment in an area that one is passionate about or continuing to grow in one's career. Managers can then create an environment for employees in which even the needs that sit on the highest point of the triangle are met by providing challenging work assignments and an opportunity for career advancement.

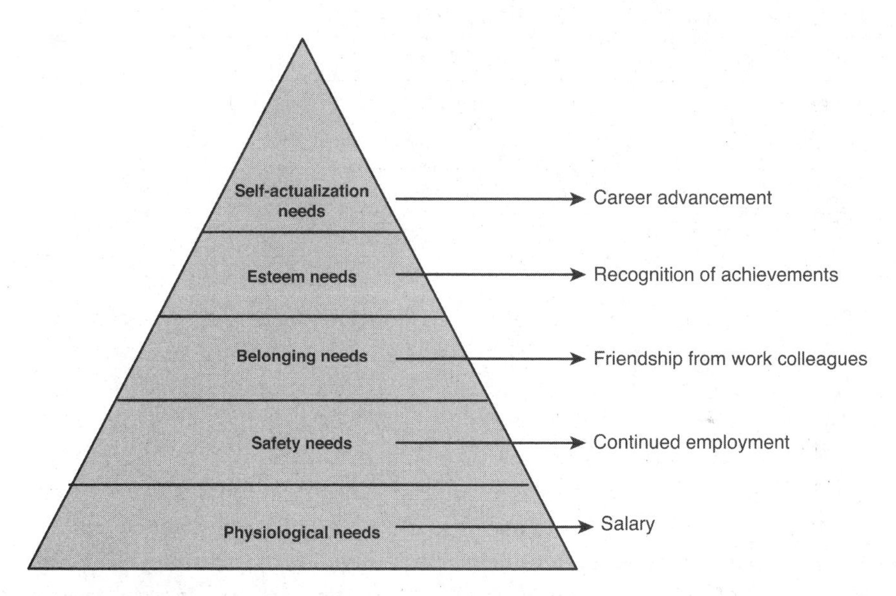

Figure 2.1 Maslow's hierarchy of needs in a work environment.

Another theory of motivation emerged a few years later; Frederick Herzberg developed the "two-factor theory" and in 1959 published his findings in a book entitled *The Motivation to Work*. He and a research team interviewed 203 accountants and engineers in Pittsburgh, Pennsylvania, about satisfiers and dissatisfiers at work. Herzberg found factors that caused satisfaction (motivators) were different from factors causing dissatisfaction (hygiene factors).[6] Table 2.1 shows the two sets of factors that caused either satisfaction or dissatisfaction and affected employee morale and productivity. Motivation factors relate to the work itself such as challenging work and recognition and provide satisfaction that leads to better morale, whereas hygiene factors relate to the work environment such as job security and salary. Hygiene factors do not give positive satisfaction, however; rather, they cause dissatisfaction if they are missing. Hence management needs to ensure hygiene factors are present—but must also provide the environment for the employee to experience motivation factors such as job achievement or career advancement.

Table 2.1 Motivation and Hygiene Factors in the Workplace[7]

Motivation Factors	Hygiene Factors
Achievement	Supervisors
Recognition	Working conditions
The work itself	Interpersonal relationships
Responsibility	Pay and security
Advancement and growth	Company policy and administration

Although both of these theories have been challenged over the years for one reason or another, they provide insight into how employees are motivated and provide management a potential framework on which to base employee career development practices.

Fast-forward to the twenty-first century, and studies continue to debunk manager perception of money being a motivator for why employees remain with a company. One study, as mentioned earlier, showed that managers believe employees leave for more money. Research conducted by Leigh Branham, along with the Saratoga Institute's surveys that included almost 20,000 workers from 18 industries and many other studies, dispute this belief. Branham says that this research revealed "that actually 80–90% of employees leave for reasons related *not* to money, but to the job, the manager, the culture, or work environment... These internal reasons (also known as 'push' factors, as opposed to 'pull' factors, such as better-paying outside opportunity) are within the power of the organization and the manager to control and change."[8]

Branham, in his analysis of unpublished research of Saratoga Institute conducted from 1996 to 2003, looked for common denominators and grouped the reasons for leaving to determine root causes. According to Branham's analysis:

"[I]t became clear that employees begin to disengage and think about leaving when one or more of four fundamental human needs are not being met:

- *The Need for* **Trust:** *Expecting the company and management to deliver on its promises, to be honest and open in all communications with you, to invest in you, to treat you fairly, and to compensate you fairly and on time.*
- *The Need to Have* **Hope:** *Believing that you will be able to grow, develop your skills on the job and through training, and have the opportunity for advancement or career progress leading to higher earnings.*
- *The Need to Feel a Sense of* **Worth:** *Feeling confident that if you work hard, do your best, demonstrate commitment, and make meaningful contributions, you will be recognized and rewarded accordingly. Feeling worthy also means that you will be shown respect and regarded as a valued asset, not as a cost, to the organization.*
- *The Need to Feel* **Competent:** *Expecting that you will be matched to a job that makes good use of your talents and is challenging, receive the necessary training to perform the job capably, see the end results of your work, and obtain regular feedback on your performance."*[9]

In fact, the number one response to the question, Why did you leave? was "limited career growth or promotional opportunity" (16% of responses), indicating a lack of hope.[10]

By now, the reader might be asking—so what do I do as a leader in an organization to improve employee engagement and therefore increase business performance? In the next section of this chapter, we discuss how IBM has used career development as a way to engage employees and increase satisfaction. Specific programs that have been implemented and lessons learned are discussed.

A Case for Change at IBM

IBM Corporation has not been immune to the phenomenon described so far in this chapter. However, by better understanding client needs, IBM has been able to develop a career framework, a structure that defines the capabilities employees need to provide value to their clients. This framework is supported by a career development process that provides guidance to employees on how to advance in their careers. But this did not happen overnight. In fact, it was only after multiple studies and an evolution of interventions over a period of years that IBM was able to achieve this goal.

The Transformation Begins

Internal surveys from 2003–2004 showed that some IBM employees felt they were not given an opportunity to improve their skills. Additionally, exit surveys revealed that perceived lack of career growth was one of the prime reasons employees voluntarily left the business. In 2004, IBM conducted a research project designed to better understand the challenges facing employees around their career development. Discussions with hundreds of IBM employees and managers, HR executives, review of existing IBM data such as exit surveys, and external benchmarking studies were reviewed. Additionally, input was obtained from an online global event called WorldJam, whereby thousands of IBM employees, managers, and executives collaborated for 72 hours and engaged in discussions on management effectiveness, workplace environment, and other matters. Collectively, input from these various studies and discussions led to a conclusion that IBM had a need for a "new day" in developing its people. These various studies pointed to five key themes that reflected the obstacles and critical success factors:[11]

- Career development is not viewed as a business priority.
- Challenging work assignments and opportunities are critical to employee development.
- Development tools are disconnected and their value to the employee is not clear.
- Career and expertise development needs to be aligned with the business strategy.
- Career development is about human interaction.

The study uncovered a huge gap between the corporate view of career development and the employee experience. Employees felt that the business focus on attaining short-term results consistently compromised development plans and activities. Furthermore, findings suggested that while many best-of-breed development resources were already available in IBM, the key challenge was that of execution. The underlying conclusion was that business priorities get in the way of development. While management can improve development practices and continue to create award-winning learning programs, in the end, none of it will make any difference unless career development becomes a business priority and employees have the time and opportunity to stretch their skills and learn new ones.

This conclusion was later validated by a 2005 study, sponsored by senior executives. The objective of this study was to recommend a strategy and implementation plan for professional development that would help IBM achieve growth and innovation and help employees attain career growth and success in a fast-changing business environment.

Based on these research findings, IBM put forth a call to action for a new day for career development that would span several years of iterative development and implementation. The new day would require redefining the roles of the employee, manager, and IBM in developing its employees and would focus the company's efforts on ensuring effective execution of development best practices. The overarching goal of the new day was to align IBM's values and business agenda with the passion of its great workforce to provide value to the client. It was about responding to employees' hunger to make a difference, to feel connected to IBM, to be recognized for their contributions, and to realize their potential. An engaged, challenged, and expert workforce would be the key to IBM's growth and innovation.

Career Programs Initiated

The following represent some of the programs IBM put into place from 2005 through 2007 as part of the first phase of this transformation of career development:

- An overhaul to the content of the new employee orientation program that had been put in place two years earlier that consisted of a 2-day classroom training and subsequent e-learning activities.

- Introduction to a one-day career event, a highly interactive, live event designed to help IBM employees learn about resources and tools they can use to grow their skills and create an engaging and energetic working experience for themselves today and into the future
- Introduction of a formal learning program that offers employees the ability to explore and participate in short-term, experienced-based learning activities available outside of the formal classroom or e-learning. It is about finding the best alternatives for personal career growth and development and then creating the optimal solution.
- Revitalization of mentoring as a way to develop skills and career development of employees.
- Developing a "one-stop-shop" website that would become the trusted source for all career development guidance and personalized learning recommendations.

Between the time the initial analysis began in 2004 through 2007, when these programs were fully deployed and functioning, IBM enjoyed a six-point gain in employee satisfaction on a periodic survey that asked employees about their satisfaction with their ability to improve their skills at IBM. While many factors could contribute to this gain, surely the significant career development programs put in place by management would have had a positive impact on employee perception—and reality.

In 2006, an IBM study conducted with clients and business partners to better understand how the company could better serve its clients revealed a need to ensure IBM employees have the appropriate skills required to provide value to the client. One of the major outcomes of this study was the need for a common career framework that could benefit all IBM employees. As a result, in 2007, IBM embarked upon an initiative to create an enterprise-wide career framework that would enable career advancement for employees. At the time of this writing, the career framework is in the process of being implemented across IBM in a phased deployment that will take several years to complete. It will ultimately support the majority of job roles across the company. This is described later in this chapter and at length in Chapter 6, "Building Employee and Organizational Capability."

The Definition of a Career Framework

Do an Internet search on the words "career framework," and you will find literally thousands of websites in which all manner of organizations—large and small, public and private—have implemented a framework to guide employees in the development of their careers. The sites will contain many common words and phrases, such as skills, competencies, training and learning, career path, career progression, succession planning, gaps in skills and competencies, capabilities, opportunities, and more. Some frameworks are targeted at ensuring employees have the critical skills needed to satisfy customer demand and/or to achieve organizational goals. Other frameworks tackle longer-range career progression challenges such as how employees cannot only serve organizational goals by growing their skills, but also how they can enrich their lives through developing their careers along a particular path or even by changing paths over time. Others view the career framework as an enabler for succession planning. The possibilities seem to be endless—and they are defined differently from organization to organization.

In this chapter, an overview of IBM's new career framework is presented, which when fully implemented, will be the backbone for how employees progress in their careers. It is also a major component of IBM's expertise management system. The framework will be supported by a structured career development process that all employees currently utilize. Subsequent chapters describe IBM's current career development process in depth and show how it provides the appropriate guidance for employees to grow the expertise needed to perform their current and future job roles. In addition, throughout the book, we highlight where applicable, on-going changes to the current career development process based on a need for continuous improvement.

The Definition of a Career

Various dictionaries provide numerous definitions for the noun "career," however "pursuing one's life work" is a common thread. According to Dictionary.com,[12] a career takes on various meanings as a noun:

> "an occupation or profession, esp. one requiring special training, followed as one's lifework: *He sought a career as a lawyer.*"

"a person's progress or general course of action through life or through a phase of life, as in some profession or undertaking: *His career as a soldier ended with the armistice.*"
"success in a profession, occupation, etc."

Merriam-Webster.com[13] offers similar definitions, such as:

"a field for or pursuit of a consecutive progressive achievement especially in public, professional, or business life <Washington's *career* as a soldier>"
"a profession for which one trains and which is undertaken as a permanent calling <a *career* in medicine> <a *career* diplomat>"

At IBM, these traditional views of a career are changing. As the technology industry continues to expand at a rapid pace and clients' IT environments become increasingly complex, today's employees need to be more multi-faceted, with a varied and versatile set of skills developed over time. No longer can a career be looked at as something that is undertaken as a "permanent calling."

In today's business arena, technical aptitude alone may not always be sufficient. There is a requirement for people to widen their portfolios of job roles, skills, and experiences to be applied and recombined in numerous ways to fuel innovative business value.

According to Ranjay Gulati, who wrote in a *Harvard Business Review* article in May 2007, "Rather than highly specialized expertise, customer-focused solutions require employees to develop two kinds of skills: multi-domain skills (the ability to work with multiple products and services, which requires a deep understanding of customers' needs) and boundary-spanning skills (the ability to forge connections across internal boundaries.)"[14]

Although a life-long career as a specialist in a particular area is still needed and valued, marketplace demands suggest that some segment of the employee population needs a wider breadth of skills. This may enable—and/or force—employees to switch career paths over time to complementary or totally different job roles where new skills must be continually learned.

A career framework can facilitate both types of progression paths, whereby employees can grow in their careers either vertically in one area of specialization or horizontally across multiple areas of specialization over the course of time. Figure 2.2 shows this vertical and horizontal career progression.

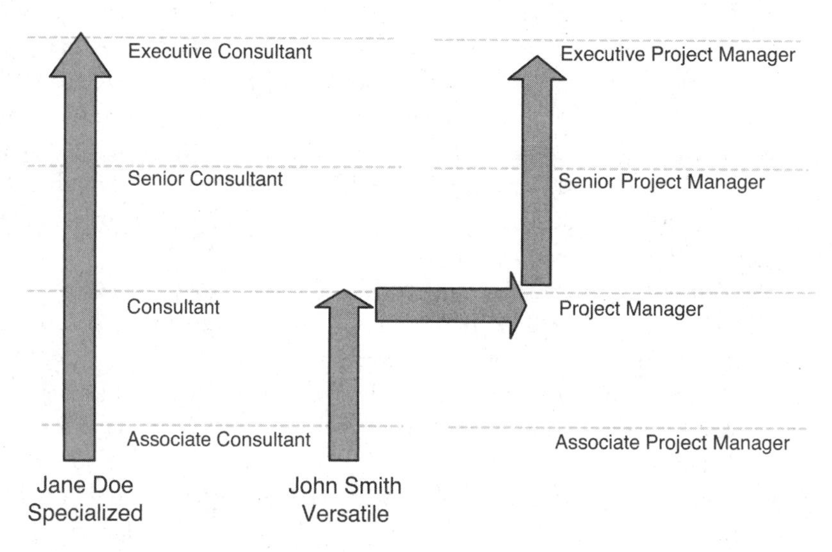

Figure 2.2 Examples of two career paths.

Figure 2.2 depicts the career path of a consultant, Jane Doe, who starts out as an associate consultant and over time continues to grow her consulting capability through working on multiple engagments, increases her expertise via formal learning and on-the-job training, and takes on more responsibility as her job position matures. At the appropriate time, as she works her way up the consultant career ladder, has many client experiences, and receives various promotions over a number of years, Jane eventually becomes an executive consultant and is recognized as an expert in her field by not only her manager and peers, but by the client as well.

It should be noted that there is not necessarily a right or wrong time period for how long it may take an individual to go up the career ladder. It is determined by the individuals, their performance, the experiences they receive, the skills and capabilities they develop, and of course, the needs of the business. It may take many years to build the right capabilities needed to perform at the next level of any particular job role.

In contrast, John Smith, although he also starts out as an associate consultant, at some point he decides to branch out and leverage the project management skills he developed as a consultant by leading client engagements. He hears that project managers are in demand, given that the company is moving toward a project-based business. He also likes the planning aspects of the consulting role and wonders if he might be suited as a bona fide project manager. He explores this with his manager, who encourages John to think about becoming more versatile in building his capabilities. John subsequently decides he wants to change career paths and actually become a project manager. He works with his manager to put an individual development plan in place and identifies the additional skills and on-the-job experiences he needs to become competitive for a project manager job role.

John completes different learning activities to increase his skill in managing projects. He also works with his manager to be placed on the appropriate consulting projects to get increased experiential, on-the-job training. Once he has built more than just a beginning level of capability in managing projects, he finally takes on a project manager role, and over time, he gains sufficient expertise as a project manager and becomes competitive for promotion. Now John not only manages the project by tracking timelines, putting work breakdown structures in place, and managing to the project plan, but given his expertise as a consultant, he also gets involved with the consulting teams in expanding business opportunities. His more versatile set of capabilities has enabled him to expand beyond the expected career path and use more of the many skills he has acquired, rather than focusing specifically on his technical abilities.

Each career starts out in a similar fashion, but eventually these two individuals follow different paths that both result in success and fulfill a need for the company, the client, and the employee.

Setting the Baseline for Expertise Management

During the 1990s and early 2000s, changes occurred that would come to have a profound impact on IBM's workforce. The explosion of the Internet and the ensuing services now needed by current and future clients to create complex networks resulted in a need for many new types of IT job roles and skills that hadn't even been "invented" at the time. Expansion in emerging markets also created unique opportunities for different types of jobs, based on the skill base of varying countries. Lastly, IBM's strategy of acquiring companies and their associated workforces and providing outsourcing services to companies—as well as hiring the outsourced company's employees—created unique niches in "instantly acquired" job roles.

A more formal structure for developing expertise became paramount to attracting, developing, and retaining a skilled workforce of over 300,000 employees that were located in all corners of the globe. It's hard to imagine the chaos that would result if there were no common language for defining job roles or the associated skills, or if each country or business unit "did its own thing," based on what it thought was needed. There would be no way for employees to know about opportunities across the company, considerable waste and duplication of effort would be required to keep independent structures in place, and total solutions to meet client needs would not be feasible.

Around 1992, IBM created its first version of a "skills dictionary" or the beginning of a taxonomy that would define the skills needed by employees. Later that decade, IBM went on to create job roles based on this taxonomy and later expanded it globally across all business units. It has emerged into what is today, an expertise management system. This system guides the identification of the following elements:

- **Competencies**—The system starts with competencies that are needed by all employees, regardless of their job role, country, or status. These competencies or behaviors demonstrated by top performers are key indicators of success for high-performing employees and differentiate IBMers from competitor companies.
- **Skills**—Employees also focus on developing skills specific for their current roles or exploring skills needed for roles to which they aspire. Skills are fundamental to specific job roles and enable employees to perform their day-in, day-out tasks.
- **Capabilities**—As employees grow their competencies, become enabled, build skills, and gain new experiences, they develop multiple capabilities that clients value.

Competencies and Associated Behaviors

Given the changing face of the IBM population, in 2003, IBM introduced competencies that were employee-focused. This was an expansion of existing competencies that were already focused on the development of leaders. There was a need to establish a common set of competencies that defined what it meant to be an IBM employee. These new competencies and associated behaviors were critical to achieving success for all IBM employees. They provided the foundation for professional growth and underscored company values, as well as established a common standard of high performance across the company. A robust curriculum of hundreds of learning activities were aligned to each of the competencies and their associated behaviors.

The competencies quickly became an underpinning of various HR processes, for example:

- The competencies are used to select new employees and as criteria for internal job movement. Various recruitment tools, including evaluation of job candidates, have incorporated the competencies as fundamental requirements of a successful employee at IBM, in addition to whatever technical or specialized skills a prospective candidate brings to the table.
- IBM's performance management system has incorporated the competencies into its annual evaluation process and has had a significant impact on how results are achieved. Hence managers must consider an employee's demonstration of the competencies when assessing year-end performance evaluations.
- The competencies have become a staple in pinpointing areas of focus that are important for individual development planning. Employees are encouraged to consider the competencies as they create their annual development goals and associated learning plans for achieving business performance.

Over time, the competencies have continued to show value to employees. Since the inception of the competencies in 2003, on average, over 300,000 learning activities in the competencies curriculum (classroom and e-learning activities) have been taken annually by IBM employees worldwide.

In a study conducted in June, 2004 by the IBM HR team, over 80 IBM employees across multiple business units participated and reported positive impact by increasing their competencies via the learning activities. Comments from participants include the following:[15]

> "I was able to use what I learned in the Adaptability course in relation to recent organizational changes."

"After taking How to Create Effective Presentations, I paid more attention when I created a presentation, which resulted in a more effective presentation."
"I learned how to look at a project from the customer's point of view. This approach made it easier to understand what they are asking for. Hopefully, this change will lead to better relationships and the ability to provide them with what they want."

While the competencies have been extremely helpful to employees in defining the "basics" of what they need to demonstrate to be successful in their jobs, at the time of this writing, IBM is going through an extensive research study to determine whether the competencies are in line with the needs of today and tomorrow's environment. The study may yield a new or refined set of competencies—or even a new structure for how the competencies are reflected in the career framework that is currently being deployed to employees.

Skills that Align to Specific Job Roles

IBM's expertise taxonomy provides a standard framework and single set of terms so managers can develop and deploy resources consistently across all geographies and business units. This also allows IBM to satisfy developmental needs based on business unit and individual requirements.

The taxonomy is "housed" in a large database that identifies job roles and associated skills, creating common terms to describe what people do across the entire company. Although this may sound like a typical job description, the taxonomy provides the foundation for many other HR processes that enable having the right person, with the right skills, at the right time, place, and cost. This common language ensures consistency across various downstream IT applications that pull data from the taxonomy. For example, one of the various processes IBM uses is an assessment of employee skills. Applying the taxonomy to this type of assessment enables the company to determine what skills are in abundance, which skills are in need, and where those skills are located. This enables placement of employees with those skill sets on the appropriate projects or client engagements.

All employees need to grow and develop their skills. Hence, being able to identify what skills are needed helps employees identify current skill needs and future job opportunities. It also provides the foundation for the types of learning activities an employee needs to progress in a chosen career.[16]

Developing Capabilities

The career framework at IBM is an integral part of IBM's expertise management system and provides the structure for how employees develop expertise over time; it also provides guidance for employees' career progression. Furthermore, a structured career development process provides the various processes, tools, and career resources employees need to grow within the framework. The process also helps ensure that employees are growing the right skills as business strategies and needs change over time.

Capabilities are core skills that can be leveraged across the business. They are based on a multitude of experiences that IBM must deliver to enable client success. Capabilities focus on what's needed to perform effectively, and they rely on a combination of applied knowledge, skills, abilities, and on-the-job experiences. Typically, multiple skills are required to demonstrate a level of proficiency in a particular capability. The level of achievement individuals attain in a particular capability is a composite of their education, skills, knowledge, and experience. To develop a capability, IBM employees must perform designated activities and achieve successful and consistent results that fulfill specified requirements as outlined in the capability level.[17] The development of capabilities provides an avenue for advancement in one's career by helping employees focus on the skills and experiences needed to advance within or move to other job roles in the company.

The career framework and supporting career development process provides guidance to employees on the variety of ways by which they can grow their careers in a linear or non-linear fashion (i.e. developing across many careers, resulting in development of multiple capabilities to varying levels). Generally, employees develop their careers at the job family level, for example, careers in Human Resources or Finance. As the career framework is deployed, employees will also be able to follow broader careers whereby employees leverage previously learned skills and apply them to new, but related job roles. For instance, a consultant is an expert in consulting methodology, however, because the consultant has to manage a consulting engagement, he also develops some level of project management skills. Over time, the consultant may desire a career change to become a project manager. He continues to grow his skills to eventually qualify for a new position as a project manager. The employee builds not only depth in a particular capability, but also breadth by growing capabilities in other complementary areas that enhance the individual's ability to deliver client value. The process facilitates educated career advancement and encourages employees to progress in broader ways.[18]

Developing a varied set of capabilities is critical in IBM's changing definition of career, where versatility in what one knows is becoming increasingly important to satisfying client demands. The primary objective is to help employees understand the core capabilities that IBM needs to deliver and what specifically employees need to do to make its clients successful. By establishing a common set of global capabilities with career milestones, the capabilities establish a common language that can facilitate career development and movement across the business.[19]

Summary

This chapter covered the importance of focusing on career development as an enabler of employee satisfaction and how development of a common career framework and supporting career development process can facilitate employee growth and progression in achieving career goals. Organizations would benefit from creating some form of framework that provides employees the ability to see the breadth of opportunities available to them and how they can grow by moving across job roles or business units. Other advantages include

- Offers employees clear guidance on how to advance in their careers
- Supplies a roadmap to developing capabilities that employees need not only to provide value to the client, but also to shape their own career paths over time
- Provides clients with employees who have the capabilities to deliver "best in class," seamless service
- Aligns with company values and desired culture
- Contributes to the company's image in the marketplace and as a company to work for

The career framework provides a model for how employees grow their expertise. A structured career development process provides the various resources employees need to advance their careers. In the next chapter, we introduce this supporting structure and provide the reader the opportunity to explore how some or all of these components may be suitable for their own organizations.

Endnotes

[1]Paradise, Andrew. "Learning Influences Engagement," *T+D* magazine, January 2008, pp. 55–58.

[2]Gendron, Marie. "Keys to Retaining Your Best Managers in a Tight Job Market." *Harvard Management Update*. No. U9806A. Copyright 1998 by the President and Fellows of Harvard College: All rights reserved.

[3]Adair, John. *Leadership and Motivation: The Fifty-Fifty Rule and the Eight Key Principles of Motivating Others*. Philadelphia, PA: Kogan Page U.S. 2006.

[4]"Maslow's Hierarchy of Needs," Wikipedia.com, http://en.wikipedia.org/wiki/Maslow's_hierarchy_of_needs.

[5]Graphic adapted from "Maslow's Hierarchy of Needs," Wikipedia.com, http://en.wikipedia.org/wiki/Maslow's_hierarchy_of_needs.

[6]"Two-Factor Theory," Wikipedia.com, http://en.wikipedia.org/wiki/Two_factor_theory.

[7]Herzberg, Frederick, "One More Time: How Do You Motivate Employees?" *Harvard Business Review* (September–October 1987), Reprint 87507, p. 8.

[8]Branham, Leigh with the cooperation of the Saratoga Institute™. *The 7 Hidden Reasons Employees Leave: How to Recognize the Subtle Signs and Act Before It's Too Late*. New York: AMACOM Books, 2005, p. 3.

[9]Ibid, p. 19–20.

[10]Ibid, p. 20.

[11]People Development Team. "People Development at IBM: A New Day" presentation. December 17, 2004: p. 9.

[12]Career. Dictionary.com. http://dictionary.reference.com/browse/career.

[13]Career. Merriam-webster.com. http://www.merriam-webster.com/dictionary/career.

[14]Gulati, Ranjay. "Silo Busting. How to Execute on the Promise of Customer Focus." *Harvard Business Review*, May 2007: p. 105.

[15]IBM Learning Team in conjunction with Productivity Dynamics, Inc. IBM Competency. *Level 3 Measurement Summary Report*, June 2004: p. 9.

[16]IBM Intranet, Expertise Taxonomy website; "About Expertise Taxonomy."

[17]Career Framework Team. Career Model Guide Playbook Chapter. March 24, 2008. p. 2–4.

[18]Career Framework Team. Career Model Guide. December 31, 2007: p. 48.

[19]Career Framework Team, March 24, 2008, op. cit. p. 2–4.

Chapter 3 Contents

3

Defining the Career Development Process

Introduction

An architectural drawing for a new home provides the schematic of constructing the house. It provides a floor plan, that is, the layout of the rooms and various components that need to go into the house to make it structurally sound and built to the buyer's specifications. But it doesn't tell the builder how to go about building the house. The builder needs a process for how to approach construction. For instance, the ground upon which the house is built must be prepared prior to laying the foundation of the house. And the foundation must be laid before construction of the walls begins, and so on. In other words, a building process, step-by-step, is required to ensure that the house eventually reflects the architectural drawing.

The builder and the buyers may spend innumerable hours going through the floor plans to ensure the buyers get exactly what they are paying for. The builder then creates a plan for how construction will begin, what resources will be used, and when those resources need to be available for each step of the process. If any of these steps is skipped, the construction of the house could falter.

Career development is similar in many regards. The career framework, as described in Chapter 2, "Enabling Career Advancement," provides the architectural drawing of an employee's career. It provides the "floor plan" of the different job roles and experiences one may need to pursue. Similar to building a house, career progression can't happen haphazardly. There are steps that should be logically followed—steps that are part of an overall career development process that leads to building a career. The various steps work in tandem to create a structured approach to achieving career goals; however, any good career development process should have enough flexibility built into it so that employees have choices as to how they progress through a particular career path based on business needs and personal aspirations.

Employees want to grow in their careers. We saw in the previous chapter that employees leave a company for a variety of reasons, citing career opportunity as one of the highest motivators for seeking work elsewhere. Hence even the smallest of organizations need to provide some form of career development process to ensure employees can identify skills they need to do their jobs, to remain engaged, and to be competitive for other positions.

What Is Career Development Anyway?

According to the National Career Development Association (NCDA), the founding division of the American Counseling Association (ACA), " 'Career development' is the total constellation of psychological, sociological, educational, physical, economic, and chance factors that combine to influence the nature and significance of work in the total lifespan of any given individual.... NCDA policy is that the key word in the concept of career development is work that represents the need to do—to achieve—to know that one is needed by others and is important. Work is a major way for individuals to recognize and understand both who they are and why they exist" within the context of the personally meaningful and satisfying contributions they make to society. The NCDA policy goes on to say, "It is when people regard what they are doing as work that productivity is maximized. Without work, the best a job can provide is economic security benefits—which may not be enough to motivate an employee to perform in a maximally productive manner. The goal of career development is ensuring that the individual finds work, as well as a job."[1]

It is important to understand what drives work satisfaction. Managers reward their employees, but then employees leave anyway. Managers believe they did all they could to prevent the departure—but they stop short of really understanding what drives employee behavior. That's where they're wrong. According to a Harvard Business Review article written by Timothy Butler and James Waldroop, "What's often missing from top performers' jobs are responsibilities that coincide with their 'deeply embedded life interests.' These are more than hobbies or enthusiasm for certain subjects—they are long-held, emotionally-driven passions that bubble beneath the surface like a geothermal pool of water....These interests don't determine *what* people are good at; they drive the *kinds* of activities that make people happy. Thus, people keep returning to these interests throughout their lives—even though they may not be fully aware of how the interests are subtly influencing their career decisions. A manager can help uncover an employee's life interests by probing, observing, and applying a little psychology. That done, manager and employee can customize work with job sculpting, a process that matches people to a job that allows their deeply embedded life interests to be expressed."[2]

IBM takes a holistic approach to career development, which encompasses processes that consider business needs as well as employee desires. The process identifies the skills needed by the company to achieve its mission. It also helps employees determine what they want to do with their work—where their deeply embedded life interests are—as well as showing them how they can achieve such goals at IBM through career progression.

The purpose of IBM's career development process is to enable employees to acquire, develop, and apply the skills needed to drive business results, while providing them with the opportunity to advance and grow their careers. Career development at IBM is designed to create an organizational climate in which employees can realize their potential through opportunities to perform work that is both challenging and stimulating. IBM places significant value on continuous career development for employees. In fact, IBM continually assesses the need for investing in new resources that help guide employees in their career development. For instance, the career framework that was described in Chapter 2 is currently being implemented at the time of this writing. It is being deployed to several targeted groups of employees in IBM as part of a phased implementation approach, either replacing or improving upon prior frameworks. The career framework will eventually be expanded throughout the company as part of a longer term strategy to have all employees using one common career framework. Hence as the needs of the business and the environment change, IBM continues to improve and reinvent its career development processes and supporting IT applications. This focus is critical to IBM's success in the marketplace and to providing value to its clients.[3]

The Benefits of Career Development

IBM's career framework and supporting career development process offers many benefits to employees, managers, clients, and shareholders as described in this section. Most, if not all, of these benefits would be equally applicable to other companies. As a company implements a career framework and a supporting career development process, it is important to identify the benefits to the various constituents. The benefits can be used to "sell" the idea of implementing a career development process to senior leadership so the investment can be secured. The benefits can also be used in communications to managers and employees to create excitement and "buy-in" as part of the implementation. The benefits are also important to clients and shareholders (if applicable); if they see that the company has invested in ensuring their employees have the skills to serve client needs and therefore create client satisfaction, it benefits the client and ultimately shareholders.

Benefits to Employees

Employees have much to gain by engaging in career development. If the process is implemented properly, it provides employees the guidance and resources they need to advance in their careers. Career development also provides other benefits including the following items:

- It enables employees to identify and take advantage of opportunities to stretch and develop market-valued skills that are aligned to both the company's business strategy and the employees' interests and passions.
- It helps employees identify which job roles are in demand and where those jobs may be located, as well as which are no longer needed. Hence

the process provides employees a view of job expectations so they are able to focus on realistic development plans.

- It offers employees a process through which they can have meaningful career discussions with their managers and/or mentors. Employees need support as they continue on their career journeys, so it is critical that they form relationships with managers and mentors who can provide that support.
- It provides visibility to areas in which expertise is needed across the organization. Hence, the process provides an avenue for employees to transfer to other job roles across the company by using a common career development process, career framework, and other resources.
- It helps employees be better equipped to provide value to their clients.

Benefits to Managers

Managers play a key role in supporting their employees' career development. It is the manager who guides employees on career development. The manager can influence an employee's decision or enable the appropriate network to ensure the employee is exposed to the right experiences needed to achieve career goals. Managers also benefit from the company having a career development process and overarching framework. These benefits include the following items:

- The career development process helps managers guide their employees through career progression. The process helps managers determine what skills are needed, what job roles are required, and which employees may be best suited to fulfill those job roles.
- A career development process shows employees that the company values their growth and development, and thus it could be a valuable retention aid. This would save the manager time and money that are drained from high rates of attrition. The reduced turnover will also help increase client satisfaction.
- The process facilitates talent planning by identifying where skill gaps and gluts may exist. This assists managers in determining where to invest in skill development or where they may need to hire additional resources.
- Career development helps to maintain a vital, engaged workforce that leads to increased morale, employee (and ultimately client) satisfaction

and retention. This can assist managers in achieving their organizational goals.

- Career development helps to shape a more skilled and flexible workforce that can meet client demands.

Benefits to Clients

Clients are the recipient of a successfully implemented career development process. When employees of the selling company have the appropriate levels of capabilities required to serve clients, these clients procure products or services that will better satisfy their needs. Other benefits include the following:

- A company that uses a career development process yields a more highly skilled employee. Thus, clients have better insight into the type of service or product they are buying, based on who is serving them from the selling company.
- A better-skilled employee could yield fewer product or service defects, resulting in greater client satisfaction.
- A better-skilled employee is able to develop superior, more cost-effective solutions to client needs.

Benefits to Shareholders

Shareholders also benefit from a company's career development process, which signals that the company invests in its workforce. This benefits shareholders in a variety of ways:

- An investment in career development leads to a more skilled workforce, which in turn, yields to a higher quality service or product. This strengthens the company's market image and increases shareholder value.
- Investing in career development is a good business practice. It signals to shareholders potential strength in leadership, which is a valued quality that shareholders typically look for in a company.

Flexibility Needed in Career Development

Career development at IBM is a partnership among employees, their managers, and the company. IBM's culture provides the environment for individual growth and for an IBM career that is rewarding to employees. The company is committed to strengthening the manager-employee relationship in order to help employees optimize their performance in and satisfaction with their jobs. The manager is required to take an active role in employee development; however, employees must take personal responsibility by continuing to develop their skills in a way that adds value to IBM and its clients. This can be accomplished through the multi-step career development process that all IBM employees engage in with their managers, and which leads to the benefits described in the preceding section. Although the process is structured with a recommended sequence of activities, it is agile enough to allow for diversity. Diversity has been a long-standing strategy in IBM that gives employees an appreciation of how individual differences create a culture that fosters innovation. IBM's career development process supports diversity and takes into account many differences, including organizational differences, learning style differences, employee needs, changes in company strategy, and demonstration of company values. This agility is paramount to the success of any career development process. It cannot be so rigid that it doesn't account for individual needs at the organizational or individual level. Examples of these differences are described in the following sections.

Organizational Differences

The course of employee development is often determined by the different products or services provided by the various business units across a company. At IBM, on the one hand, there are employees such as consultants or project managers who provide services and who often move from one short- or long-term engagement to another. Employees such as these often need a versatile set of skills in order to provide service to many types of clients. These employees might require different learning paths, and/or certifications to maintain their skills to remain competitive.

On the other hand, manufacturing employees or engineers who work on the creation of product have "static" work environments. They typically do not move from client to client or even engagement to engagement.

They support the manufacture of a particular product and are often specialists in its production. Their learning paths are very different from employees who provide services. Certifications, if required, may be more process- or product-related.

Learning Style Differences

Adults often have different learning styles; some can read a book or instruction manual and be able to perform the activity, whereas others need a hands-on demonstration of how to do it. Still others are able to learn from various types of self-study e-learning, although their preferred learning style may be in a more collaborative environment. These style differences are further compounded by cultural and generational differences.

Some countries and cultures prefer—and even demand—a more collaborative environment for learning. The type of learning provided for such countries may have to be more classroom or collaborative-based than would be necessary in other cultures.

It is also important to understand the values of the different generations that are now found in the workforce today. According to organizational development scholar, Dr. Morris Massey, "If we examine the value system shared by generational groups then we can better understand their diverse beliefs and behaviors." Dr. Massey goes on to say that it is important to "understand the mind-sets of different generations and how each group sees the world based on their experiences."[4] It then becomes critical to understand what motivates members of different generations and to institute teaching techniques that are flexible enough to meet their needs.

Employee Needs

In a world where four generations of employees might well be sitting side-by-side with different needs and desires as to their careers, flexibility in how these employees are developed is mandatory.

Employees close to retirement age may be deep experts in their fields and have reached their ultimate levels of capability. They are still highly productive workers; however, their career needs are going to be very different than those of new employees who have just joined the company—and the workforce. Seasoned employees may need to learn some new skills as the work changes. They often accomplish this in innovative ways, using informal learning methods that may require very little help or support from their manager. They also seek help from peers across the company, using the networks they've created over the years.

However, new employees fresh out of college have not yet made the kinds of networking connections to other company employees that their longer-term colleagues have, so these younger workers look to their managers to guide them in navigating the company. New employees are also eager to progress—often rapidly—in their careers, but they don't always know what path might be the best approach for them. Therefore, the career development process must support both tenured, experienced employees who might only need to focus on a few skills, as well as brand new employees with little experience, who could require extensive training, mentoring, and job changes over time in order to advance in their careers.

Strategy as the Driving Force Behind the Career Development Process

IBM's corporate strategy drives the particular skills employees need to do the jobs required to achieve the company's goals. As corporate strategy changes over time, so must the workforce strategy, including the types of employees hired, the jobs they do, and the skills they need. The career development process plays a critical role in enabling the company to determine what expertise the company has—or doesn't have—to meet new challenges. This helps determine where to invest in employee training to ensure that the company has the expertise necessary to meet client demands. It also helps managers set career expectations with employees to guide them in growing required skills. In addition, the career development process provides an avenue for employees to advance in their careers in a way that is meaningful, motivating, and exciting. A career development process can help managers level-set with employees on realistic career goals and can be used as a positive lever in employee retention.

IBM Values as the Foundation of How Employees Act and Develop Themselves

Enterprises stand the test of time based on a foundation of core values. In 2003, IBM re-examined its values through a rigorous yet dynamic approach. According to IBM's internal website, "Through ValuesJam—an unprecedented 72-hour discussion on the global IBM Intranet—IBM employees, managers and executives came together to define the essence of the company."[5] The result was a set of core values that shapes everything the company does and every choice made on behalf of the company. This shared set of values helps employees make decisions and, in the process, shapes the company. But the real influence of these values occurs when employees apply them to their personal work and their interactions with other colleagues, clients, and others around the world. IBM Values therefore provide a foundation for how employees should carry out business and develop themselves.

Traveling the Road to Career Development

Each employee's path to career growth is unique. Employees themselves can decide where they want to go in their careers and the best way to get there that's right for them, keeping in mind the need for balance with business requirements. Certain job roles may no longer be needed, and new job roles may emerge. In addition, not all employees are able to advance to higher levels within the company either because they do not possess the right type of skills or the business does not have such a need. Employee expectations must be aligned to company needs. Thus the career path employees take is driven by their aspirations and abilities, as well as the organization's business needs.

Figure 3.1 shows the elements that help yield a meaningful career in IBM. The sections that follow provide a closer look into how these various elements work in tandem.[6]

Company Business Strategy and Goals

IBM's strategy targets the intersection of technology and effective business. According to IBM's internal website, "Today's networked economy creates a new economic landscape and a mandate for business change. IBM's strategies are designed to help its clients be successful through information technology and services."[7] As the company strategy changes, so must the job roles that are required to execute that strategy. Employees must keep their skills in alignment with these changes. As part of the annual performance management cycle, IBM employees identify their business and development goals early in the year. Employees identify the business goals required to achieve the organizational goals

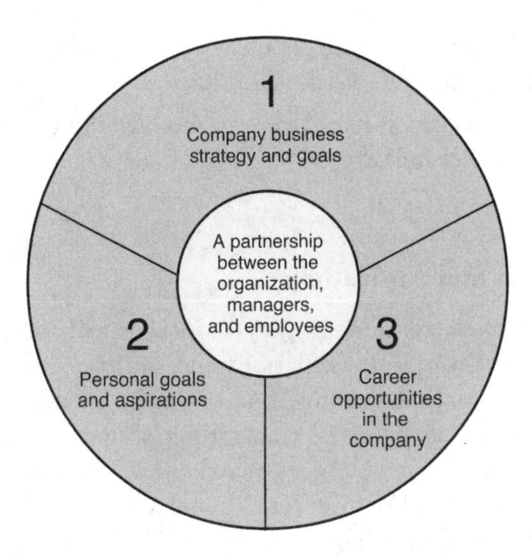

Figure 3.1 The elements of career development

that align to IBM's corporate strategy. The ongoing ability to meet these goals is used as an evaluation criterion at the end of the year when managers report on how well employees performed against the goals they had set. Additionally, employees identify development goals and learning activities that will strengthen the skills needed to help them achieve their current-year business goals.

As employees explore their development goals, IBM provides them with guidance to help them define these goals. The following are some thought-provoking questions related to IBM strategy that employees should consider in setting and achieving their business goals:

- What is the company strategy?
- What is your business unit's strategy, and what are your business unit's priorities?
- What role do you play in executing the strategy?
- What are the market-valued skills for your business organization?
- How can you best help your manager and your organization reach their goals and priorities?
- What role do you play in executing your business unit's strategy?
- How have business needs and technology evolved, and do you understand them?

- What is important to your clients today, and how does your job role support your clients' business needs and priorities?
- How do you see your job role changing, and how can you best prepare yourself for these changes?[8]

Personal Goals and Aspirations

Throughout their careers, employees periodically need to re-assess where they're at. Over time, situations and personal desires change. As an example of a situational change that drives career decisions, take Jane Doe. She joins IBM as a business transformation consultant, with several years of related experience. She is married but does not yet have any children. By joining IBM as a consultant, she can fulfill her current desires to work on consulting engagements. This often requires that the IBM consulting team be physically located at a client site. This lifestyle requires frequent business travel, which in Jane's current situation, suits her. Over time, however, Jane eventually starts a family. She now has to re-evaluate her situation. Frequent business travel does not allow her to be home during the week. As the children grow to be of school age, she would like to be able to participate in their activities, so Jane decides that she'd like to pursue some different career options by exploring other IBM jobs that utilize her consulting skills, but which do not require such heavy business travel. At some point in the future, as Jane's children age, she might take yet another turn in her career as her personal situation changes.

This is only one short example of the many changes that can impact one's career. An agile career development process needs to provide a way for employees to explore their aspirations over a period of time, re-evaluate, and even change jobs as situations or desires fluctuate. A flexible career development process helps employees explore what they're passionate about, what skills they have or need to grow, and who and what can help them achieve their goals.

Career Opportunities in the Company

As IBM defines the job roles needed to execute upon its strategy, it provides potential career opportunities for its employees. IBM offers resources to employees to define the expertise they need in their current jobs or for future aspirations. Employees need to consider whether their career goals are realistic based on their skills and the needs of the company—and to reset those expectations if they are not realistic. This requires that employees take the time to reflect on what their strengths and current expertise are, what they really like to do, and how this aligns to company needs. It is often helpful to think of past job activities or assignments that were fulfilling and that the employee has been passionate about. Employees should also talk with their manager and/or a mentor to get a better perspective on career opportunities at IBM. This leads to a vision of what a job in IBM might look like for that individual and could help define the career goals needed in order to attain the job. Employees should document these goals for a discussion with their managers as they identify their development goals for the year. Here are a few questions that employees use to identify their career development goals and career aspirations:

- What words would you use to describe your capabilities and personality?
- What are your strengths, and what tasks do you do well naturally?
- What types of jobs or roles do you most enjoy, and why do you think you enjoy them?
- What are your work and life balance goals and priorities?
- How do these goals align to the needs of the business? Are they realistic goals?[9]

A Partnership Between the Organization, Managers, and Employees

Employees need to determine what their career desires are within the context of a partnership among the employee, the organization, and the manager. They need to achieve a certain level of performance, and the organization is responsible for ensuring the right learning environment and career development opportunities so employees can keep their skills razor sharp. Managers need to work with their employees on setting career expectations and helping them achieve realistic career goals.

A formal career development process provides the appropriate checks and balances needed to ensure that employees are not led down the wrong path. It provides guidance on what job roles are in demand—or are no longer required. It also provides guidance on how to achieve career goals. It is the manager's responsibility to work with employees to understand their career desires in light of the needs of the business and to set employee expectations. It is also the manager's responsibility to approve development plans and learning activities that the employee wishes to take. Managers also must approve job rotations and promotions. Hence it is important that employees work with their managers to ensure that the right career expectations and plans are set.

The Career Development Process: An Overview

Where should employees begin? How do employees determine which job roles and careers to seek; and once determined, how do they grow levels of expertise that will help achieve business and personal goals?

In the remainder of this chapter, we provide a brief description of the steps in IBM's career development process. This offers a holistic view of the career development process at the macro level. Each subsequent chapter is then dedicated to providing further details, including examples, best practices, and more illustrations about the intricacies of each step of the career development process. As an introduction to this holistic approach, a chapter-by-chapter view of IBM's career development process is summarized in Figure 3.2.

Selecting and Developing New Employees

At IBM, career development begins even before a new employee walks in the door. IBM has identified competencies that are characteristics of people who demonstrate outstanding performance. IBM's competencies have been established through rigorous research to differentiate high performers from average ones and to establish a common standard for high performance across IBM. The competencies include personal characteristics such as knowledge, skills, social role, and motives that enable behavior. They describe behaviors that IBM employees should possess and exhibit to effectively deliver client value, be effective leaders, and demonstrate the IBM values. Competencies are broadly applicable across IBM and are key capability enablers.[10]

IBM takes these competencies into consideration as part of its recruitment process for prospective new employees. According to IBM's

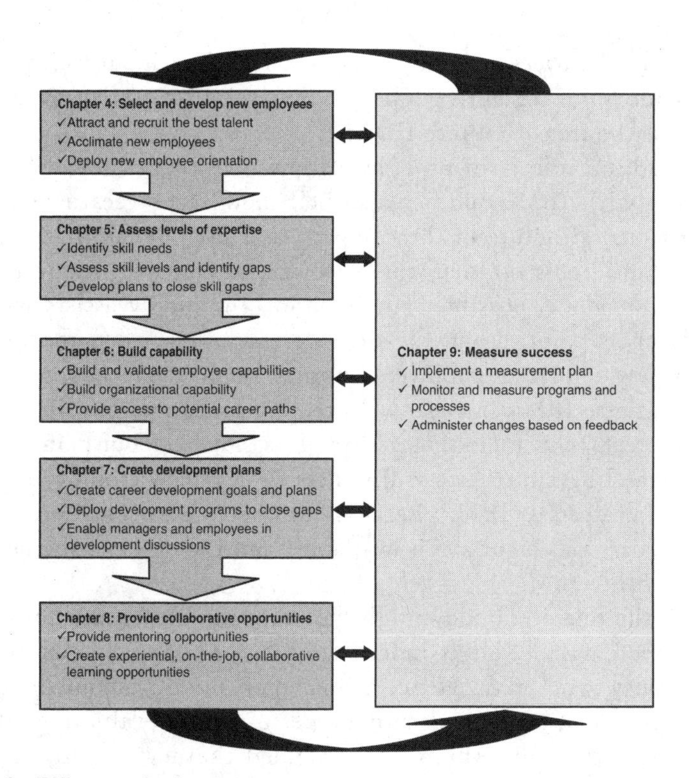

Figure 3.2 IBM's career development process.

Behavior-Based Structured Interview Reference Guide, "The activities and requirements of the job are matched with the knowledge, skills, abilities, and values described in the competencies." The Guide goes on to say that, "Subject matter experts, including managers and employees, confirm that the competencies reflect critical requirements for success on the job."[11] The competencies provide the framework for interview questions and rating criteria for interview guides. This enables hiring managers to identify and make offers to applicants with the right qualifications who will help IBM meet the challenges of the Information Technology market.

After candidates have been selected for hire, their prospective managers assign them a "buddy," even before they join IBM. Consistent feedback from new employees has emphasized the importance of having a buddy when the new employee joins IBM. Creating an early connection to IBM helps retain top talent, which is a win for the new employee as well as for the business. The buddy gives managers the opportunity to match new employees with experienced ones who can answer questions and provide guidance during a new employee's first 60 days, thus helping to ease the transition into IBM.

The buddy's role is to provide insight into the values and culture associated with IBM. Buddies also help new employees navigate the organizational structure of the company and become familiar with key websites and tools so that the new employees are productive and engaged as soon as possible. Furthermore, the buddy assists with the basics, such as pointing out the site cafeteria, explaining processes, and giving newly-relocated employees information on the local area.

According to IBM's internal website, managers need to select as buddies volunteers who are enthusiastic and passionate about being an IBM employee and have a sincere willingness to help new employees as they begin their careers at IBM.[12] Because the buddy is assigned prior to the employee's arrival, he or she is available from the onset of the new person's entry into IBM.

While the role of a buddy might not be a significant amount of time for any one employee, it is indeed time he or she must take from an already busy work day. Hence a manager should acknowledge the buddy's role as part of the annual performance evaluation plan to acknowledge the value the buddy provided the new employee. IBM's experience in talking with former new employee buddies has shown this to be a very valuable experience for the buddy. They often report it is a very rewarding experience to help a new employee, and often these initial relationships end up being lasting friendships.

New Employee Orientation Program

Employees begin their careers at IBM by attending a new employee orientation in a continuum of learning. While the orientation provides the basic information employees need to be productive at the company, it is more than just a class. Rather, it is a mandatory orientation program that introduces new employees to the history, culture, values, and strategic vision of IBM. Successful completion of the program has been proven to lead to improved early career success for new employees. Interviews with new employees has revealed that the program provides new employees faster integration into IBM, faster project deployment, more effective collaboration, and higher overall satisfaction with joining IBM. In addition, a study comparing participants to nonparticipants over a two-year period revealed that a higher percentage of attendees received a top performance rating, compared to those employees who did not attend the program. The study also showed that more attendees would remain with IBM, even if offered comparable jobs and salaries elsewhere.

The orientation program begins with a classroom experience and continues with an e-learning program and "Touchpoints" that span the employee's first year, to help new employees become successful in their careers. The following list provides a high level description of the various components of the program:

- The *classroom component* offers sessions on company values, culture, business environment and strategy, as well as productivity-enhancing tools and processes.
- The *online learning plan* consists of various phases of e-learning, featuring self-paced modules and mastery tests on a variety of important topics and tools to help new employees learn about IBM's values, processes, culture, tools, expectations, and career development. Monthly progress reports, including links to manager/employee discussion guides, are sent to new employees and their managers to help to ensure that new employees receive the support they need during their first year.
- *Touchpoints* provide on-going live and recorded presentations via conference call by the company's foremost subject matter expert on a given topic. Following these are Question and Answer sessions that help build knowledge and skills by delivering valuable information just when new employees really need support during their critical first year.
- The *New IBMer Zone*, an internal website, provides very useful information for new employees and their managers.[13]

The program is used by all hire types, including university/college hires, professional hires with years of experience, employees who are part of company acquisitions, and experienced professionals who become IBM employees through strategic outsourcing deals.

Once new employees complete the program, they then follow the same career development process that all IBM employees follow. As outlined in Figure 3.2, IBM's career development process includes a variety of recommended and some mandatory steps that employees follow, typically on an annual cycle. However, these steps are flexible and will vary based on a variety of factors, including but not limited to tenure with the company, personal aspirations, current and prior level of expertise, business goals and needs, level of employee, and job role.

This description outlines IBM's new employee orientation program, which has been in place since 2003. It is important to note that the program has gone through various transformations over time to reflect changes in the types of new employees being hired, the needs of new employees, market conditions, company strategy, and various other factors. In fact, at the time of the writing of this book, the program is going through yet another transformation to reflect the needs of tomorrow's new employees. We will further explore the current program details in Chapter 4, "Selecting the Best Talent and Developing New Employees," as well as highlight upcoming changes.

Assessing Levels of Expertise

As employees meet with their managers to discuss their annual business and development goals, employees need to consider what skills they need in order to achieve their business goals. If there are gaps in the required skills, the development plan can help identify the learning that needs to occur to close gaps. IBM has initiated the Expertise Assessment to help employees understand development needs. The Expertise Assessment is based on IBM's Expertise Taxonomy, described in Chapter 2. It is a process IBM developed that allows employees to assess their skills for their current job roles against a target level of mastery for each skill. Managers then review and approve the assessment. The ideal time to complete an expertise assessment would be early in the year, as employees are creating their annual business and development goals. This provides a foundation for the current year's development plans.

Employees can also view target skill levels needed for other job roles to which they want to aspire and can also do a self-assessment to identify future skills they may need to acquire. The Expertise Assessment provides information about the individual's job role, associated skills, and a list of associated skill development activities that can help the employee advance in his or her career, while meeting the business needs of IBM. Once an assessment is completed, IBM employees are able to identify the gap between their current skill levels and their expected targets. This step is critical for employees to understand the areas of development that would improve their effectiveness as employees. In most cases, learning is available to close those specific gaps.

Expertise Assessments are important for a variety of reasons:

- To help employees develop and execute a plan to attain skills and achieve career advancement.
- To help IBM match employees with assignments and to align their skills with IBM's business strategy.
- To help IBM be more efficient and more competitive by supporting its most valuable resource...its employees.
- To help employees get the right training for each skill, personalized learning is available to address individual skill needs or gaps.[14]

Growing Levels of Capabilities

In the previous section, we outlined the processes used to identify skills needed for a current or future job role. Expertise Assessments are very important, as they focus on the individual skills necessary for success in one's current job role or even future job role. Skills can be developed in a relatively short period of time. The focus shifts, however, as employees increase their skill levels and move from job to job. They ultimately grow levels of capability that lead to achieving a significant milestone in one's career. Capabilities require a combination of applied knowledge, skills, competencies, or other characteristics, and are developed through experience. Capabilities are a core element of IBM's career framework, as described in Chapter 2 and are necessary to drive client value and advance an employee's career. Capabilities can take a relatively longer time to build. The two programs complement each other and provide a broad overall perspective on how employees can develop themselves and their careers over both the short- and long-term.[15]

Creating Meaningful Development Plans

The expertise that an employee grows is a key building block for developing a professional career. However, to set a direction and prioritize the goals employees want to achieve, they need a plan. As employees define their development goals early in the year, they also document their plans for development. This includes identifying the learning activities that help employees close skill gaps.

This necessitates a discussion between managers and their employees. The discussion that employees have with their managers regarding their development needs and plans is critical to ensure that the manager sets appropriate expectations related to employee career goals. Some employees may find that their long-term goals are unrealistic and have to make different choices. For instance, employees may desire to become executives in the company, but they might not possess the right types of skills or have the appropriate executive characteristics. In this case, the manager needs to work with the employee to ensure that the chosen career path matches the employee's capabilities. The manager also approves the learning activities identified by the employee. The manager may have to suggest other alternatives if some learning activities are not available or achievable.

When the plan is reviewed and approved by the manager, employees then execute the plan throughout the year. Having well-thought-out plans greatly improves employees' abilities to attain their career goals, but success also depends on acting on the plans, and monitoring progress.

Supplementing Development Plans with Experience-based Learning

Learning activities can take on many formats, from formal classes and e-learning, to readings and experiential on-the-job learning. While IBM employees have the opportunity to partake in formal learning, they also have the opportunity to gain new skills by learning on the job.

IBM provides a formal experiential learning program designed to help employees take advantage of a range of experience-based learning opportunities such as stretch assignments, cross-unit projects, job rotations, and more, which will enhance their careers and expertise. "Opportunity" in this context refers to the many ways in which IBM employees can utilize the resources available to them, enlist guidance from fellow IBM employees from across the business, and leverage experience-based activities to both enrich their careers and adapt to the demands of a rapidly changing marketplace.

This formal program provides structure and guidance for managers on how to create unique opportunities that may help the managers achieve their mission, as well as meet employee needs and help shape development plans. Getting involved doesn't require a huge commitment on the employee's part. Opportunities can range from as little as a few hours, to one day per week, to several months.

IBM also has a very robust mentoring program open to all employees. Mentoring has become a hot topic in IBM and many other business organizations today. Competition and changing technologies are putting pressure on businesses to make improvements in cost, quality, speed, and service at rates never required before. Organizations are realizing that they must become "learning organizations" to enable quick deployment of employees throughout the business to respond to these pressures. Mentoring is an important tool in the development of the learning organization. Mentoring joins two or more people together to achieve specific objectives for skills growth and development. Simply put, the mentor has the skills, knowledge, and experience that the mentee needs.

At IBM, the mentor agrees to share this know-how and act as a role model. The mentee agrees to make a conscientious effort to acquire the development offered by this program. A mentor can have more than one mentee, and a mentee can have more than one mentor.[16] IBM's mentoring program is anchored on three pillars:

- **Organizational Intelligence**—Mentoring is a tool to bridge leadership gaps and gaps in knowledge. Mentoring makes the company a knowledge-resilient enterprise. This places the company in a position to have the right knowledge base that is necessary to offer creative solutions to the market that IBM serves.
- **Connecting People**—Mentoring connects people on many levels and removes barriers that inhibit collaboration. Employees can more easily connect across geographies, business units, and across diverse cultures.
- **Business Impact of Mentoring**—Mentoring has the power to better engage employees and foster a climate of on-going learning. As employees collaborate through mentoring and develop new skills, the company is better able to deliver quality products and services to its global clients. Other business benefits include increased morale and having employees who feel a sense of value to the business.

Measuring Success

An organization can invest millions of dollars in developing its employees, but at the end of the day, how do organizations know that the investment has paid off? IBM has a very robust measurement process that leverages Donald Kirkpatrick's four-level training evaluation model.[17] In addition, IBM uses various internal surveys to capture employee opinions on its learning investment and career development processes. These surveys include

- An *internal trended survey*, which takes place periodically throughout the year to provide more frequent, relevant feedback from IBM employees. It is a high-level sample survey with benchmark comparisons to other companies. It provides information on employee satisfaction and key workplace climate topics that drive satisfaction and business performance.[18]
- A *workplace effectiveness survey* is given annually and captures employee opinions about career development resources, in addition to other work environment factors.
- Surveys ask employees to rate their satisfaction with individual online applications for effectiveness. These applications might include the electronic learner management system for enrolling in training, the online purchasing system, or other online tools employees use to do their jobs.

These various data points collectively provide ample input back to management to make improvements to the learning activities and career development process.

Summary

In this chapter, we explored the many advantages of career development and also outlined how IBM approaches its career development process to enable employees to grow in their careers. While the practices shared are approaches that work in IBM, there are many facets of IBM's career development process that could equally be applied to other organizations. Here are a few key points to keep in mind:

- Career development is a structured process; however, it needs to provide enough flexibility to take differences into consideration and to allow for those differences in approaches to career development. These include organizational differences, learning style differences, employee needs, company strategy, and company values.
- Managers need to support employees in enabling career development, but managers also need to guide employees to ensure their career goals are not unrealistic. Employees have a responsibility to take the initiative to

act upon development plans—their careers are their careers, and they have to own and manage them.

- Career development can open doors for employees—and organizations. It can act as a motivator to retain employees, saving companies turnover time and money.

The remaining chapters in the book further explore the concepts introduced in this chapter. Each chapter is dedicated to one or more of the career development process steps as outlined in Figure 3.2.

Endnotes

[1]National Career Development Association Board of Directors, Career Development Policy Statement. Adopted March 16, 1993; revised 2008, p.2, http://www.ncda.org/.

[2]Butler, Timothy and Waldroop, James. "Job Sculpting: The Art of Retaining Your Best People," *Harvard Business Review OnPoint*. President and Fellows of Harvard College, 2002.

[3]IBM Career Development Team. "Managing Your Career—Employee Perspective: Basics," February 11, 2008. p.2.

[4]The National Oceanographic and Atmospheric Association Office of Diversity. Tips to Improve Interactions Among the Generations. Traditionalists, Boomers, X'ers and Nexters: http://honolulu.hawaii.edu/intranet/committees/FacDevCom/guidebk/teachtip/intergencomm.htm.

[5]IBM Intranet. About IBM website; "Values," October 30, 2006.

[6]IBM Career Development Team. "What's New in Career Development? Employee Overview," 2008. p.4.

[7]IBM Intranet. IBM Strategy website: "Strategy," Updated May 12, 2008.

[8]IBM Career Development Team, "Managing Your Career," loc. cit, p.3.

[9]Ibid., pp. 3–4.

[10]IBM Career Development Team. "Working Careers and Capabilities Glossary," May 2, 2008.

[11]IBM Recruitment Team. "Behavioral Based Structured Interview Reference Guide," 2003. p.6.

[12]IBM Intranet. You and IBM Website, "Employment—IBM Connections," Updated March 27, 2008.

[13]IBM Lotus Notes. Invitation to the New Employee: "Overview of Your IBM for Managers and Employees."

[14]IBM Intranet, Expertise Taxonomy Website; "Expertise Assessment."

[15]IBM Intranet, Career Framework Website. "Overview: Question & Answer," Updated September 2008.

[16]IBM Mentoring Team. "Mentoring: The Basics," March 19, 2008.

[17]Kirkpatrick, D.L. (1994). *Evaluating Training Programs: The Four Levels*. San Francisco, CA: Berrett-Koehler.

[18]IBM Global Pulse Survey Team. You and IBM—Global Website: "Learning More about the Global Pulse Survey," Updated October 18, 2007.

Chapter 4 Contents

4

Selecting the Best Talent and Developing New Employees

The Changing Landscape for New Employees

Over the past decade, dramatic changes in workforce dynamics have compelled organizations to take a different view of recruiting and onboarding practices. When correctly implemented, such changes offer companies the opportunity to gain competitive advantage. What these organizations need to do first is understand the dynamics that are changing the face of the workforce and then establish and/or tailor recruiting and onboarding practices and programs accordingly. A number of factors contribute to this changing landscape.

First of all, the scarcity of talent has been a major concern of business leaders, as noted in two *McKinsey Quarterly* global surveys. In 2006 at the time of the survey, which polled more than 10,000 respondents, business leaders indicated "finding talented people as likely to be the single most important managerial preoccupation for the rest of this decade." The second survey on organization, completed by more than 1,300 executives in November 2007, "revealed that nearly half of the respondents expect intensifying competition for talent—and the increasingly global nature of that competition—to have a major effect on their companies over the next five years. No other global trend was considered nearly as significant."[1] That, however, must be weighed with the environment caused by the economic crisis that erupted in 2008.

Massive layoffs across many industries, corporate bankruptcies and store closures, and mergers and acquisitions of many companies have now created a dynamic where more and more individuals are vying for fewer jobs. In addition, many companies have scaled back on ambitious hiring programs. While more talent may be available for jobs, there could be a mismatch of available talent. Individuals who are seeking new jobs as a result of the economic crisis might not have the appropriate skills needed for those jobs that are available. On the other hand, new industries, such as "green" companies and products, will arise that will create jobs and demand different skills than may have been seen in the past. Displaced employees from other industries might need to learn different skills for these new types of jobs. Hence companies need to reassess their staffing needs in light of the financial debacle that began in earnest in 2008 for not only current conditions today, but for when the economy turns around in the future and hiring demands increase. This will also cause companies to reevaluate their career development programs and processes to ensure they keep pace with workforce needs.

Another factor is that in the United States, baby boomers, born between 1946 and 1964,[2] are attracting a great deal of attention. According to the U.S. Department of Labor, *Bureau of Labor Statistics News* published in December 2007, total employment is projected to increase 10 percent between 2006 and 2016. The labor force filling these jobs will not only be more racially and ethnically diverse, but is also projected to grow more slowly than in the past. Part of this slowdown in growth is due to the aging and retiring of baby boomers. "The number of workers in the 55-and-older group [during this 10-year period] is projected to grow by 46.7 percent, nearly 5.5 times the 8.5 percent growth projected for the labor force overall."[3] This condition could potentially create a significant number of additional job openings. However, on the flipside, the global economic crisis of 2008 and beyond has the potential to create yet another situation where baby boomers remain in the workplace longer than anticipated to catch up on lost savings to retirement accounts. More flexible workplace arrangements may need to be made to accommodate the needs of an older workforce.

Then there is the explosive growth in emerging countries such as China and India, which has created a huge need for hiring often very young workers in large quantities and at a rapid pace, in order to keep up with new job openings that are being created.

Factor into the equation the introduction of Generations X and Y (those born between 1965 and 1975 and between 1976 and 2001, respectively[4]) to the workforce, and we see the need for a dramatic shift in the approach to selecting *and* retaining the best talent in the marketplace. Unlike the baby boomers (born between 1946 and 1964) who preceded them, Generation X and Y workers often don't adhere to traditional concepts such as employee loyalty or long-term tenure with one employer.

Generation Y, sometimes referred to as the Echo-Boomers, the Millennials, the Trophy Generation or Trophy Kids, or the Net Generation, among other names, is the group of people born anywhere between the second half of the 1970s and the mid-1990s to around the year 2000, depending on the source.[5] This group offers a particular demographic challenge. According to an article in the *McKinsey Quarterly* published in January 2008, Generation Y's world view has been shaped by a number of factors, including "the Internet, information overload, and overzealous parents. HR professionals say these workers to demand more flexibility, meaningful jobs, professional freedom, higher rewards, and a better work-life balance than older workers do. People in this group see their professional careers as a series of two-to-three-year chapters and will readily switch jobs, so companies face the risk of high attrition if their expectations aren't met."[6]

People have more complex needs than a paycheck and a workstation. They are affected and motivated by whether they feel valued by the company, whether their skills are appreciated and fully leveraged, and whether they feel challenged, fulfilled, and recognized for their contributions. According to Kaiser Associates, Inc., new recruits are looking beyond their early tenure at their new company; they are looking at what companies are doing to address their early career development needs, how quickly and easily they are able to become familiar with company culture and performance values, their ability to develop friendships and social connections, and the ease with which they're able to handle the basic administrative needs associated with becoming a new employee.[7]

The structures of companies are also changing—in some cases with little or no forewarning. Unprecedented changes related to the financial turmoil in 2008 caused a record number of mergers and acquisitions of large financial institutions. This resulted in members of Organization A becoming new employees of Organization B overnight. Additionally, companies such as IBM use well-thought out company acquisitions to quickly fill critical skill gap needs. These strategies lead to two different cultures merging, a "marriage" that needs nurturing and caring so that productivity by the acquired company does not falter.

According to Kaiser Associates, Inc., a 2006 global study of more than 3,700 job seekers and 1,250 hiring managers, conducted by Development Dimensions International and Monster Intelligence, states that "32 percent of corporate employees who have been in their current job less than six months are already job searching."[8] Dissatisfied new employees can quickly become disengaged, significantly reducing their discretionary effort in the form of extra time, energy, and brainpower. They "down-shift" their naturally hardworking pace because they do not sense that anyone in the company cares. Equally harmful, they can have second thoughts about their job choice and be open to the opportunity to move companies. This is extremely costly to the company, not only in terms of the financial and personnel resources invested throughout the recruitment and onboarding processes, but also in terms of productivity lost and the compounding error of sending a newly trained employee straight into the arms of a competitor, not to mention the damage to a company's reputation of being an unreliable prospective employer.

Taking these dynamics into consideration when planning onboarding programs is the natural next step after mutual talent and employer selection. Effective onboarding and orientation approaches can help new employees navigate a company's complex processes, policies, tools, and culture. These programs can help new employees feel connected to the business and understand how their work contributes to the company's success.

In this chapter, we provide insights into the overall onboarding process, including a review of the selection process that helps ensure a match between company and prospective employee expectations, and success factors for onboarding new employees and for what to do in the months thereafter. We share examples and lessons learned that IBM uses to 1) recruit via a structured interview process that focuses on employee skills and competencies needed for the job and 2) subsequently acclimate new employees through its robust new employee orientation program, with well-documented evidence of the positive results for the company's bottom line, as well as for employee engagement, satisfaction, retention, and productivity.

Actions for Onboarding Success

In the talent management universe, the new employee orientation and mainstreaming process is known as "employee onboarding." According to Brian Platz, Executive Vice President and General Manager of SilkRoad Technology (www.silkroadtech.com), in an article for About.com, he says, "Keeping in mind that companies never get a second chance to make a first impression, your business should make absolutely sure that new hires feel welcomed, valued, and prepared for what lies ahead during the new employee orientation or onboarding process."[9]

Each "wrong" selection decision can be costly in terms of managing an employee that has been disillusioned or who doesn't possess the appropriate skill to do the job, and even more if one factors in lost opportunity cost with clients. Hence, companies need to implement recruitment and selection processes, and subsequent onboarding programs that align the expectations of both the company and the job incumbent.

According to Kaiser Associates, Inc. having such on boarding programs "have become strategic tools by which companies are able to differentiate themselves from their recruiting competition."[10] If the company's screening and selection process is robust enough, a new employee will start a job with the correct skills needed to succeed in that role, augmented by an initial excitement about the future. But if new employees are treated in ways that demonstrate a lack of preparation for their arrival, inadequate direction or training for their tasks, perceived ineffectiveness in handling their questions as new employees, and indifference or an unwelcoming attitude from their managers, they may quickly become disenchanted and fail to form a close bond with their new company. Without appropriate training on navigating the complexities of the new company's business landscape and culture, new employees can feel stifled.

Since the early 2000s, IBM has hired thousands of new employees worldwide, with a critical need to select the right skills. Its mix of new employees is very diverse in terms of the number of countries where hiring occurs, the types of hires that come into the company via various sources, and the physical location of these new hires.

IBM has a significant global presence. According to the 2008 IBM Annual Report, IBM operates in over 170 countries, with approximately

65 percent of its revenue located outside the United States.[11] Employees at IBM and its wholly owned subsidiaries totaled 398,455 in 2008 and increased 11,897 from 2007. The United States remained the largest country, with about 115,000 employees; however, about 71 percent of its workforce was located outside the United States, with increases in Asia Pacific and Latin America. "The company continues to add resources aggressively in emerging markets, particularly in the BRIC countries—Brazil, Russia, India and China—where employment totals approximately 113,000."[12]

Many of IBM's new employees therefore come from outside the United States, and they include all levels of experience, from new college graduates to experienced professionals with years of industry expertise. Another group of IBM's new employees come through strategic or business transformation outsourcing deals in which IBM takes over specific operations of another company, whose employees become IBM employees. From 2000 to 2008, IBM acquired over 100 companies,[13] which also added significantly to its employee base. Lastly, about 40 percent of IBM's employee population work remotely and beyond the confines of a traditional IBM office, such as from a home office or a client site. Bringing new employees into an environment where work colleagues are not co-located creates a need for special attention to ensure the new employee does not get "lost" or feel isolated. Each of these hire types has different needs and expectations that must be addressed as part of the onboarding process.

As companies study the dynamics that are changing the workforce landscape and design new onboarding programs and supporting processes or enhance existing ones, a number of critical success factors come into play. These factors are instrumental in selecting the right employees and quickly acclimating them into the company so that they achieve high levels of productivity early in their tenure. This not only benefits the company, but also helps the new employees achieve work satisfaction and meet their career goals and expectations. Based on IBM's experience of providing formal onboarding programs over the past decade, these critical success factors include the following:

- **Executive support**—For any onboarding program to succeed, it has to be supported by senior management. Executives at the highest levels of the company must take the concept of onboarding new employees seriously and treat it as a business imperative. They have to provide adequate funding to design, develop, deploy, and maintain the program and act as advocates to ensure the entire organization "buys in" to ensuring its success.

- **Requirements**—The program needs to be reevaluated on a continual basis. Therefore, gathering requirements from managers, employees (particularly those that have been recently hired), and executives is key to ensuring that the program meets the needs of the various constituencies. It is also important to talk with leaders from different business units across the company to ensure their unique requirements are part of any onboarding program.
- **Cultural differences**—If a company is global, it must understand the cultural differences and needs of a global audience. What works from a training perspective in one culture might not be as effective in another culture.
- **Mandatory attendance and completion**—Whatever formal aspects of the onboarding program are deployed, attendance in and completion of the program must be mandatory. To ensure all new employees have ample time to acclimate to their new environments, onboarding programs cannot be optional.
- **Holistic approach**—Successful onboarding is more than just attending a class on Day 1; it is a holistic program that includes many facets from the day the person is recruited to months after the first day of work, when the new employee ends the "honeymoon period" and strives to meet longer-term career goals.
- **Customization**—One size does not fit all when it comes to onboarding programs. The needs of university hires with little or no job experience will be much different from those of 20-year industry experts who may have worked for multiple companies during their careers. Local cultural preferences need to be considered. That is, because some cultures are more collaborative than others, online learning may have nominal impact for employees who are used to high levels of collaboration. Furthermore, employees who did not necessarily choose to join the new company but were brought in either through an acquisition or merger, will have different needs than a recruited employee who made a conscious decision to join the company. This is coupled with generational differences as mentioned earlier in this chapter. Trainers must understand these various audience types and create an orientation program that is flexible enough to allow for audience differences. It should be noted however, that each

audience doesn't necessarily need its own orientation program. All new employees need to learn about "core" knowledge, including the company's strategy, its culture, policies, processes, and other information. When there are audience differences, attention must be given to determine if customization is required.

- **Content design**—It is important to involve content design specialists in the design of the program to ensure that requirements are met and needed customization follows learning design standards. A well-crafted program designed by instructional experts, particularly for complex environments where multiple aspects of the program need to be customized, will yield a more pointed program that will truly meet the needs of the different audiences.
- **Measuring success**—Even the best onboarding programs need to be constantly measured and evaluated to ensure they are meeting the needs of new employees. Quickly changing environments and workforce dynamics leads to a continual need to update and even overhaul new employee orientation programs and onboarding practices. Measurements that determine not only program effectiveness and relevance, but also the impact on the business will help garner support across the entire organization. Benchmarking against other organizations ensures that onboarding programs do not become stale and allows the firm to leverage other company's best practices.

Selecting Talent

According to an article by Laurie Friedman in the November 2006 issue of *T+D* (Training and Development) magazine, "Recruitment efforts bring potential hires to your door, but how well your organization manages the interview process will influence whether the candidate takes the position. It also provides the candidate with a long-term impression of your organization. The first impression can create a lasting impression, so make the most of that first meeting. Additionally, there are several crucial questions that need to be answered prior to the candidate's arrival, such as: What will potential new hires learn about your company during the interview process? Are they kept waiting prior to meeting the hiring manager? Are employees friendly and welcoming? How is information shared about why your company is a great place to work?" Even if the candidates themselves are not hired, they may refer other potential candidates, and the company would want the referral to be a positive one.[14]

Any unique characteristics of the job should be explained to the candidate. These characteristics may be positive for some candidates but negative for others. For instance, a job might require significant travel. That could be appealing to some candidates; however, other candidates might not be in a position to travel for significant periods of time due to their personal situation. All aspects of the job should be explored during the interview process so there is a clear understanding of job expectations before an offer is made by the company or accepted by the candidate. Once the new employee is in the door, what was promised in the interview needs to become real. An onboarding program can help build this bridge.

We begin by exploring the first two components in the sidebar on the next page, "A Checklist of Actions for Bringing on New Employees," which are related to recruitment and selection. To ensure that the best possible candidates are hired and ensure linkage to skills and competencies important to the company, IBM uses a refined behavioral-based interviewing process that has been successfully used in other large companies. This is a competency-based, structured approach to interviewing that focuses on an applicant's past behavior and experience, which is an indicator of future performance.[15] It gives managers and other interviewers a clear roadmap for selecting better candidates.

According to Katharine Hansen, Ph.D., creative director and associate publisher of Quintessential Careers™, "The premise behind behavioral interviewing is that the most accurate predictor of future performance is past performance in similar situations. Behavioral interviewing, in fact, is said to be 55 percent predictive of future on-the-job behavior, while traditional interviewing is only 10 percent predictive. Behavioral-based interviewing is touted as providing a more objective set of facts to make employment decisions than other interviewing methods."[16]

In fact, one reason the structured approach works is that it focuses on the applicant's behavior. In the behavioral-based interview, the applicant is asked to provide examples of behaviors from his or her past experience. Behavior is defined as evidence of what a person has said or done (or failed to do) in a given situation. For instance, if the candidate is applying for a project manager job role, the hiring manager is interested in determining whether an individual can perform project management tasks, what they actually can do and how they did such to achieve successful results. Typically, the questions are open-ended so the manager can get complete information on how the candidate handled themselves

CHECKLIST OF ACTIONS FOR BRINGING ON NEW EMPLOYEES

Based on IBM's experiences with onboarding new employees, the following is a "checklist" of actions companies should consider to ensure their recruitment and onboarding programs and processes are effective:

- ✓ Align job expectations during recruitment so new employees are not disillusioned after they begin work.
- ✓ Link skills and competencies important to the company to the selection process.
- ✓ Once an offer is made, welcome the prospective new employee and provide critical information he or she will need early on—before getting in the door.
- ✓ Ensure the manager is supportive of the new employee prior to Day 1 by having the employee's working environment ready, including the workspace, computer equipment, and other essential work tools or resources needed to be productive immediately.
- ✓ Introduce new employees to their work colleagues; make sure the colleagues have responsibility for acclimating and helping the new employees.
- ✓ Assign a "buddy" to help the new employee navigate the company.
- ✓ Provide formal, mandatory new employee orientation training early—beginning on Day 1 or 2 preferred—that includes both an in-person component and subsequent e-learning and experiential learning activities.
- ✓ Set the employee's business goals within the first 15 to 30 days.
- ✓ Introduce new employees to internal online forums, chat rooms, blogs, or other social networking resources that will help them meet other employees, particularly when employees work remotely.
- ✓ Introduce new employees to the company's career development process early in their tenure—within the first 120 days is preferable—and start to charter their career paths.
- ✓ Ensure the manager checks in with new employees often.
- ✓ Measure and monitor the onboarding programs to ensure they continually meet the needs of new employees.

in a given situation. Examples of questions the manager could use to determine a candidate's ability to manage projects might be as follows:

- Tell me about the most challenging project you have managed.
- Describe a situation you have been in when you were faced with an uncooperative project team.
- Describe some techniques you have used to increase the productivity of the project team.[17]

Probing situations such as these will provide the manager a view of the candidate's past performance and provides insights so the manager can assess whether the candidate was actually able to manage projects.

In contrast, in a more typical interview, the manager might ask general questions that only capture the candidate's viewpoint and do not demonstrate that they actually have the skills they're being hired to provide. Typical traditional interview questions might be as follows:

- Tell me about yourself.
- Tell me about your strengths and weaknesses.
- Tell me about the skills you possess to manage projects.
- Have you managed complex projects in the past?

Questions of this nature will lead to general, even subjective, statements by the candidate and do not illustrate whether the person has been able to demonstrate the skills they supposedly possess. Additionally, the last question in this second list could lead to a simple yes or no response, which does not provide any useful information to the manager.

Behavioral-based interviewing benefits include assuring that the employees hired have the right skills for their jobs and are well-suited to their roles. Reliability is increased by using a consistent approach. This more effective hiring leads to both significant cost savings and an enhanced reputation in the marketplace.

At IBM, the behavioral-based interviews center around the concept of competencies. The activities and requirements of the job are matched with the knowledge, skills, abilities, and values described in the competencies. Subject matter experts, including managers and employees, confirm that the competencies reflect critical requirements for success on the job. The selected competencies provide the framework for interview questions and rating that are provided to interviewing managers.[18]

Once an offer is made, the onboarding process begins, which is covered in detail in the next section. Examples are used from IBM's experience with new employee orientation over the past decade.

Onboarding New Employees

A formal onboarding program has a big impact on employees. It lets them know that people care about them, teaches them about the company, its culture, its values, and what it stands for and helps them learn how to get in contact with resources. It can have an extremely positive impact on morale and on how an employee views the new company. The need for onboarding programs is important from many perspectives, as is shown in Table 4.1.

Table 4.1 Needs of Onboarding Programs

Employees Needs	To better understand the company, its values, business strategies, organization, and the critical "must do's."
Company Needs	To ensure that employees are acclimated quickly so that they can become productive and effective at what they were hired to do.
Client or Customer Needs	To feel that they have providers with the best skills possible working on their behalf.

The Evolution of IBM's Onboarding Program

In the late 1990s, IBM embarked upon an in-depth analysis to enhance its onboarding efforts. Stakeholder interviews with new employees, managers and executives, as well as other studies provided anecdotal evidence of positive differentiation between employees who participated in onboarding versus those who had not. At the time, onboarding consisted of a class, held on the first two days of employment. Maintenance of the program was primarily decentralized, which meant that each business unit determined what it wanted to include in the two-day program, how it would be administered, and whether their new employees would even participate in the program. This led to inconsistencies in how new employees were acclimated and what they were taught. Eventually the employee orientation process became repetitive, inconsistent, and inefficient.

In the early 2000s, IBM's business environment started to change. More and more new employees were being hired in emerging countries outside the United States. IBM was earning increasing revenues from strategic outsourcing, a process whereby IBM provides IT support for clients. The company also introduced Business Transformation Outsourcing, which transforms and provides a client's business process in areas such as human resources, procurement, customer care, and finance and administration. Often employees of the client joined the IBM workforce as part of these deals. Additionally, IBM was now aggressively acquiring companies as part of its strategy to quickly gain skilled resources and potential market share. In fact, its largest acquisition came in 2002, when it acquired PwC Consulting, the global management consulting and technology services unit of PricewaterhouseCoopers. Overnight, more than 30,000 employees from various countries joined the ranks of IBM.

It became clear that the existing two-day program would no longer meet the needs of such a changing new employee population, nor would a decentralized approach work where each country or business unit created their own versions of the program. In fact, extensive research yielded significant input to the creation of a new program. Wide-ranging discussions with IBM executives, managers, and new employees yielded the following concerns:

- Two days of orientation training was not adequate.
- New employees didn't have a "go to" person who could answer basic questions.
- IBM's intranet was a great resource but was overwhelming to new employees.
- Many new employees were remote from their manager and their peers.
- New employees didn't feel "connected" to the company.[19]

As a result, a total overhaul of IBM's onboarding program was completed, and in May, 2002, IBM deployed its new employee orientation program called *Your IBM*. As IBM instructional designers pored through research, best practices inside and outside the company, and input from internal studies, they came to several conclusions about how to change the company's onboarding program. One of the first major assumptions was that onboarding needs to begin prior to the employee's first day. Another was that the company's values must be instilled right away and must be memorable so that new employees quickly confirm they had made the right employment choice.

According to Mel Kleiman, managing partner of the Hire Tough Group, which specializes in proven approaches to employee recruitment, selection, and retention, "Orientation should be geared toward reinforcing new employees' 'buying decisions.' The focus must be on convincing them they made the right choice when they signed on." Kleiman, also author of *Hire Tough, Manage Easy—How to Find and Hire the Best Hourly Employees*, believes that employers have to address what's foremost on employees' minds. "These are the same issues that worry kids on their first day of school each year: 'Will they like me?' 'Will I be safe here?' 'How hard is the work?' 'How will I be graded?'"[20]

In addition to first-day reactions, according to Craig R. Taylor, Senior Vice-president of Marketing and Business Development at TalentKeepers, and a contributing editor of *T+D* magazine, "Longitudinal research on employment patterns reveals what most experts agree are three fairly definable periods in the employee lifecycle, in which the risk of voluntary turnover is highest." The first phase is the initial 30 to 60 days with the new company, where proper acclimation is key. The second phase is after 1 year to 18 months on the job. Productivity may be up at this point but the new employee may have certain expectations that may or may not be met. The third phase, according to Taylor, is after 3 years, when career growth expectations emerge. If expectations are not being met, the company is at risk of the new employee leaving the organization.[21]

IBM instructional designers and other onboarding experts considered not only changes to the Day 1 class component, but also introduced a preboarding component, and a continuum of learning activities and other support mechanisms that would span the employees' first year. Resources were centralized, best practices were determined, and the global program was rolled out consistently throughout the company.

The next section offers an in-depth description of the various aspects of *Your IBM*, the onboarding program IBM has used since 2002. The program has gone through several major changes since 2002 to keep up with changing dynamics and a continual need to refresh the curriculum as company policies and practices change. In fact, every year or two the program is reevaluated to ensure it keeps pace with employee and company needs.

At the time of this writing in 2009, the program is going through another transformation to meet the needs of an evolving new employee workforce. This new version of the program is a result of extensive recent research from new employees, managers, and executives. One of the components that is under development is how IBM extends the new employee orientation beyond the first few months and to reflect a more holistic "new employee experience" that spans the employee's first two years. These changes are discussed later in the chapter.

Lastly, a robust measurement strategy helps to provide input to the reevaluation process. Specific examples related to the *Your IBM* program are further described in Chapter 9, "Measuring Success."

Orienting and Developing New Employees

IBM's *Your IBM* onboarding program that had been in place since 2002 has various components that begin when the prospective candidate accepts the position at IBM. Once the individuals begin work, they participate in a multi-faceted orientation program that spans the new employee's first year. This next section provides details of this program including the following components: pre-hire education, the new employee orientation program, and periodic "Touchpoint" calls. In addition, we cover the role of the manager and the new employee's buddy.

Pre-Hire

After the selection process is complete, new employees should be interested in better understanding the company and its business, its benefits, and policies in a more intimate way prior to their official start date. At IBM a pre-hire website offers them the ability to get connected to the company, provides them some basic information that will be useful during their first few weeks at the company, and also offers valuable information for family members. While information may vary by country, typical information contained on the website includes such topics as:

- An overview of the learning program, including the objectives and operational aspects of the workshop and the subsequent learning activities
- Tips for getting started with completing the required forms needed on Day 1
- A pre-hire checklist to ensure new employees have all the information they need to begin work, where to report, and other useful administrative information
- What to expect on their first day at work

- What to expect in the first few weeks and months, with a focus on how to connect with other company employees
- A description of the buddy program
- Information on the employee benefits, medical plan choices, and career development
- Company values
- Guidelines for conducting business
- General company information
- How to order business cards so that the cards are ready as soon as the employee begins work
- Other local country content

New Employee Orientation Program

The comprehensive orientation and development process for all IBM employees begins on new employees' first day and continues through their first year at the company. All new employees—independent of hire type—engage in the *Your IBM* learning program for new employees, however, the workshop is customized based on hire type and in some cases business unit and country location. For these customized versions, there is core content that must be included to ensure consistency across the company, but flexibility is allowed to remove or add certain topics, depending on local need. Its key elements are

- A workshop during their first week of employment, which varies from one to two days, depending on hire type
- Introduction to a comprehensive new employee website (different from the pre-hire website described earlier) that provides easy access to all the resources new employees may need and is customized with their own learning and development plans for the first year
- A personalized online learning program that provides the next level of orientation to be completed over the next several months
- A series of Touchpoint webinars or e-meetings on topics that are important to new employees

The purpose of the program is to provide a holistic learning program to new employees so they quickly become acclimated to IBM's values and legacy, which are the foundation of IBM's business goals and strategies, and to provide the tools, tips, and advice that will guide new employees toward becoming successful IBM employees. Activities and discussions are planned around IBM's values and business strategy, as well as how to effectively collaborate within the IBM matrix.

The program is designed to help new employees learn about the company and provide on-going support throughout the employees' critical first year at IBM. The program explores the company's history and its plans for the future so that employees can gain a broader context and deeper perspective of the organization.

The learning program blends online and face-to-face activities that help new employees learn about the company, connect with other IBM employees, and begin to grow their careers early in their tenure at IBM.

While the program is a view of an onboarding program that meets the needs of a new IBM employee, the components covered in the entire continuum—both the live workshop and e-learning components—should be considered as potential content for any company program. Through extensive research over the past decade, program topics have proven to be of value in quickly acclimating employees to their new work environment for maximum productivity.

The *Your IBM* workshop was designed not only to impart important information, but also to help create a learning community so that participants learn from instructors and guest presenters, as well as from one other. Employees often form a special bond with other new employees whom they meet in their first two days of orientation. The workshop typically includes topics such as the following, but the topics are customized based on hire type and in some cases by business unit and country:

- **IBM leadership through the years**—A historical view of how IBM leadership and strategy has evolved since inception.
- **Company values**—A strong connection to the company's values and how these values drive employee behavior in conducting business and maintaining relationships.
- **Company strategy**—A view of IBM's strategy and how the new employee would fit within that strategy. This topic is often covered by an IBM executive in the workshop, bringing additional insights to new employees early in their tenure.
- **Matrix**—IBM is a highly matrixed organization, with employees often taking work direction from one or more managers or project managers

beyond their immediate supervisors. The workshop helps new employees understand this matrix, how to work within it, and how to maximize the relationships and organization configuration they will encounter as a result of a matrixed structure.

- **Benefits**—Highlights of the benefits offered to all employees, including but not limited to health and life insurance, vacation and personal day policies, sick leave, flexibile work practices, employee services, and retirement planning.
- **Compensation**—Highlights of the overall compensation program, including the salary program, year-end bonuses, and other rewards.
- **Career development**—An overview of IBM's career development process and how employees need to work with their managers and potential mentors early in their tenure to make the most of their career advancement. This module includes a discussion of the annual business goal setting and year-end performance appraisal process, as well as the individual development planning process for creating a personal career plan.
- **Workstation setup**—If appropriate, new employees are provided a laptop computer during the workshop. The employees are given basic instructions about their new laptops, including hardware and software "how to's."
- **Tools and resources**—An overview of IBM's intranet, with a focus on those websites that are most beneficial to employees early in their tenure, as well as different IT applications they will need to process travel expense accounts, purchase supplies, find information on other employees via the corporate directory, and other useful items.
- **Next steps**—Employees leave the session with an action planner of things to do in the subsequent 30, 60, and 90 days and beyond, so that their first year is impactful and productive. This includes an introduction to the next component of the learning program, i.e., the personalized online learning component and the periodic Touchpoint calls.

In addition to this classroom experience, learning is provided to the new IBM employee via a new IBM employee website, which when initially developed in 2002, began as a well-organized and comprehensive source of relevant information and resources for the new employee. From a central portal, new employees accessed new employee information and resources, career development guidance, corporate strategy, company values, competencies needed, recommended books, and much more. Today, with the introduction of *Your IBM+*, the website has evolved into "The New IBMer Zone," designed to help new employees easily find vital information, connect with helpful coworkers, and begin to build a sense of their IBM communities. For example, it provides new employees direct access to details about IBM's business strategies, professional development, innovation initiatives, and productive online tools. The new employee can also receive customized development plans based on how long he or she has been with the company. Blogs, Wikis, social networking, and Web 2.0 innovations help new employees share knowledge and experiences with other IBM employees. There's even a way to connect with other new employees hired at the same time. The New IBMer Zone is one of the most frequently visited websites on IBM's intranet.

In addition to providing information and resources, the website is also the portal for the employee's online e-learning program and planning tool, which begins with a four-phase series of key e-learning activities that all employees historically have engaged in during their first few months with IBM. New employees use an online tool to create a personalized learning plan composed of certain required and optional topics based on what is relevant for the particular employee. These topics are reviewed by the New Employee Experience team at least once annually for relevance and change over the course of time as new company practices, policies, and programs are deployed throughout the year.

At the time of this writing, the online e-learning program and post-orientation support described here is being updated in the new *Your IBM+* program to reflect on-going support needed by new employees throughout their first two years versus just their first few months. This will reduce the "overwhelmed factor" reported by many new employees and provides employees what they need when they need it. Work-based and virtual learning activities provide active employee engagement in the process, and any "traditional" e-learning that remains in the program has been reduced in size/length to increase "consumability." Designed to enable integration and alignment with business unit, job role, and geography-specific learning targeted at specific segments of the new employee population, the post-orientation learning and development activities expand the use of other "players" and programs in the new employee's daily life such as his or her buddy, a mentor, peers and colleagues, and manager.

Touchpoint Calls

Another important part of the orientation and development process is a series of Touchpoint sessions, which are webcasts and e-meetings throughout the employee's first year on important, often timely, topics for new IBMers. More than 9,500 employees participate each year in these calls on topics such as The Power of Mentoring, Manager/Employee Collaboration, Professional Development at IBM, Working Effectively on a Team, Setting Your Goals, Understanding Compensation, and Your 401k. Replays are available on the New IBMer Zone website, and surveys show a high satisfaction rating.

Engaging Managers in the Process

In Michael Kroth's book *The Manager as Motivator*, he writes, "Employees inevitably point up when asked why the workplace is such a miserable environment. It's the boss, they say, or their boss's boss who makes it a depressing place to work. There is only so much you can do about the management chain, but my question to you is, 'Are your employees pointing their fingers upward at *you*?' A manager has more opportunity than any other organizational influence to directly motivate an employee. He or she has the most power to set the department's organizational climate. Managers set the tone, translate organizational strategy into employee performance and developmental plans, provide the clearest link between rewards and punishment, and in virtually every other way stimulate...employee action more directly than any other force can."[22]

This is even more critical for a new employee, who has made few connections in their first months and must rely on the manager for some of his or her very basic needs. From the beginning, managers are encouraged to reach out and welcome their new employees into the IBM culture. One of the biggest success factors that new employees cite as instrumental to their early development and acclimation at IBM is their managers and the relationship they establish with them.

The program has provided various ways for managers to get involved in their new employees' learning, thereby establishing a good rapport with them. *Manager Discussion Guides* are made available to help managers assist new employees in their assimilation into IBM. These guides are provided after the new employee exits the orientation workshop and are meant to work in conjunction with the e-learning; discussion topics and exercises are recommended to help the managers be actively engaged in the new employee's learning. This helps the managers in the employee's acclimation to the company and allows a formal time when employees can ask clarifying questions. Managers automatically receive monthly updates on their employees' progress in completing the online learning.

Helping New Employees Beyond the Learning

A buddy who helps with both business unit and job-specific information is assigned to the new IBM employee, whether that person is fresh from college or a professional hire with years of job experience. The buddy program is highly customized by hire type and in some cases might vary by business unit or country, based on need. For instance, employees hired through acquisition or outsourcing deals have a similar type of buddy program, but it is customized to their particular environments.

The buddy is assigned at least 10 days before the new employee's first day to ensure that the buddy is available right from the beginning of the new employee's IBM career. This buddy assists the employee in finding and learning about the essential information and people to help the employee get off to a quick and successful start, while freeing the manager from the time-consuming tasks of anticipating and answering new employees' basic questions.

The buddy helps new employees navigate the organizational structure of the company and become familiar with key websites so that the employees are productive and engaged as soon as possible. Buddies also help with the basics, such as locating the site cafeteria, explaining processes, and giving new employees information on the local area if they have recently relocated. The buddy is also instrumental if the new employee is working from home or remote from an IBM office. The buddy helps the new employee learn collaboration techniques for working remotely but yet staying connected to work colleagues.

The buddy is typically an employee who has been at the company at least two to three years and who has similar skills and career interests as the new employee. They may spend as much as 10 to 15 hours with the new employee during the first 60 days. The buddy is separate from others who may be involved with hiring and orientation, such as a mentor, trainer, or the manager. If the connection is not working for either the new employee or the buddy, the employee can be reassigned a new buddy. Employees and buddies are surveyed after the first 10 days to determine early whether the match is working.

Buddies are asked to email new employees before their first day to introduce themselves and provide their contact information. The buddy plays a large role in the new employee's first week. Following is a description of suggested roles the buddy might play in any company during the first week to ensure a fast and successful start:

- Assist manager with introductions to department members.
- Provide introductions to new team members, specific location information, and other pertinent information.
- Give a tour of the working area, including the restrooms, cafeteria, vending machines, copy rooms, fax machines, mailroom, confidential waste bins and conference rooms, if applicable.
- If the new colleague is located at a customer location, share pertinent information regarding the arrangements.
- Provide some quick tips about surviving the first few days—include local "lore and ways of the world."
- Point to useful information on working as a remote employee. Share personal experiences if applicable.
- Plan to "connect" with the new employee on a regular basis to ensure they feel comfortable with the company.
- Ensure the new employee knows where to find the buddy for urgent issues. Consider using email, phone calls, instant messaging, or face-to-face meetings.
- Provide information about new hire networks and diversity groups, as applicable.
- Hold on-going debrief meetings to ensure that new employees are comfortable with resolving issues.

A buddy assignment is typically an additional task the employee is asked to accomplish in addition to their regular work responsibilities. Employees that have been a buddy to a new employee have reported numerous personal benefits. It is a rewarding experience to be able to help new employees navigate their first few months. In addition, fulfillment of the role can be used as additional input to the employee's annual performance assessment so the employee gets "credit" for taking on this additional role.

Onboarding for Supplemental Employees

As part of IBM's workforce strategy, the company often hires supplemental employees. Supplemental employees are hired and employed directly by IBM for a limited period of time and are often hired for a specific skill they possess. Supplemental employees require some introduction to company policies, practices, and tools so they can quickly be productive, given the short-term nature of their employment with IBM. Supplemental employees are provided access to the new employee e-learning program and are given a personalized learning program based on topics relevant to them since some topics may not be required given the short-term nature of their employment.

Measuring Success

IBM's new employee orientation program uses a very robust measurement process that leverages Donald Kirkpatrick's four-level training evaluation model.[23] Employees complete surveys immediately after the initial orientation workshop, and at the 60-day, 90-day, and one-year marks. These surveys give regular feedback on the impact that the program elements are having on employees' job satisfaction; their ability to assimilate; do their jobs; understand IBM values, strategies, and goals; and to work the IBM matrix.

In addition, managers of new employees are asked to provide feedback via a survey conducted periodically over the employee's first year. This helps ensure managers give input related to the impact the program has had on the new employee.

Periodically, impact surveys, focus groups, and one-on-one discussions are held with new employees some time after their hire dates to capture additional data and application of what was learned in the training. An impact study conducted for program attendees in the United States from May 2003 to April 2005 indicates that the program had a highly positive impact on attendees when compared to new employees who did not go through the program:

- 50% greater retention rate for program attendees
- Higher annual performance assessment ratings for program attendees

In addition, the study revealed other significant results, showing that new employees who went through the orientation program

- Rated IBM higher as an employer
- Felt more comfortable understanding IBM and felt more integrated into IBM
- Were assigned to key work projects faster
- Collaborated with other IBM employees more effectively[24]

Managers and buddies are also surveyed to ensure a holistic view of measurement is collected. Output from this iterative measurement methodology is used as part of the improvement process for continuous updates to the onboarding program. Additional information on measures of success of the program is covered in more detail in Chapter 9.

The Journey Continues

This chapter has been dedicated to discussing IBM's historic approach to onboarding and new employee orientation. The orientation program and onboarding processes have continued to evolve over the last decade as changes to the business and the needs of new employees have demanded refreshing and revising the program and processes. As IBM moved into 2009, it significantly expanded its focus on new employees from strictly learning and development. The new approach is now referred to as "The New Employee Experience" and is an initiative to look at and improve all aspects of the new employees' experience, including changes to the *Your IBM* new employee learning program.

In 2008, input via a "jam session" and virtual workshop that Human Resources conducted with IBM employees, managers, and new employees worldwide provided insights into program and process changes. The results[25] are summarized as follows:

- New employees of all types are impressed with the type of information they were receiving during the orientation. However, in many instances, they are somewhat overwhelmed by the amount of information provided in their initial days with the company and expressed the need for ongoing support.

- Although the *Your IBM* program offered e-learning and Touchpoint calls following the 2-day orientation workshop, there was a need to revaluate the approach to post-orientation learning for new IBMers to ensure employees were effectively engaged and taking advantage of the content.
- In addition to the *Your IBM* learning program, a number of other learning programs are targeted at new employees based on their geography, business units, and job roles. The need arose to develop a global new employee program that was better suited to integrate with these specialized programs so that the new employee had a more holistic approach to orientation without redundancy from other programs.
- The design of new employee learning needed to enable easier and more effective customization for new employees joining the company as part of an outsourcing arrangement or acquisition.
- Innovative changes to the new employee learning design and delivery were needed to optimize learning delivery expenditures and ensure all employees had access to the program.

The input from the study provided the basis for the changes that are being implemented. IBM designed, developed, and recently piloted *Your IBM+*. This program replaces the previous version of *Your IBM* described earlier in this chapter. In addition to program changes, the team that supports the program, now called the New Employee Experience Virtual Team, changed its focus to evaluate the entire new employee experience in IBM, not simply the learning and development aspects.

Michael Cannon, Manager with New Employee Experience, Effectiveness & Success at the IBM Center for Learning and Development, says, "I can't overstate the importance of all new IBMers having access to the information and resources they need to understand the history, values and culture of IBM, and to get off to a fast and effective start from their very first days with the company. The newly released *Your IBM+*, The New IBMer Zone, and the work of the New Employee Experience Virtual Team not only provide a great orientation to our company, they ensure that throughout their first 2 years, employees have access to critical information and resources needed to succeed and thrive in the dynamic, complex and exciting company that is IBM."[26]

To ensure a consistent and integrated message throughout the two years of new employee learning activities, *Your IBM+* is anchored by four themes critical to new employees of all types: 1) Being an IBMer, 2)

Understanding IBM, 3) Collaborating across IBM, and 4) Developing myself and my career.[27]

The new program enhancements focus on several key areas including 1) identifying the main resources that help new employees become productive quickly and ensuring employees can find what they need without a lot of intervention, 2) driving a values-based culture and ensuring new employees understand the company philosophies and IBM brand, 3) better enable managers with the right resources so they can help their new employees succeed, and 4) ensure new employees have a clear understanding of how they can grow their skills and advance in their careers at IBM. The content that is taught in the new employee orientation training is also updated, with a focus on use of social networking technologies to help new employees collaborate with other IBM employees around the globe. This will not only help new employees in their day-to-day jobs, but it will give them a better appreciation of different cultures and what it truly means to work and collaborate in a global company.

The *Your IBM+* program consists of three components[28] that include the following:

- **Pre-Employment**—Learning material is provided soon after acceptance to ensure this important window of opportunity before day one with the company is leveraged to begin developing the soon-to-be employee.
- **Orientation Day**—A refreshed, one-day facilitator-led learning event as well as an option for a remote virtual facilitator-led version to ensure maximum coverage of new employees in all countries around the globe. Orientation day still provides a high touch kick off to *Your IBM+* learning activities that will follow in the coming two years for each new employee. It emphasizes IBM's culture/history/values/structure and the critical importance of collaboration and social networking to effectiveness in IBM.
- **Post-Orientation Day**—Employees are provided with on-going support throughout the employee's first two years. Work-based and virtual learning activities enhance active employee engagement in the process, and any "traditional" e-learning that remains in the program has been reduced in size and/or length.

Program measurements are also updated to reflect the new facets of the program to ensure that it stays fresh and continues to meet the needs of new employees and IBM.

Summary

Talent selection is the process of finding the right person for the right job at the right time. This means finding the right person for the company and the right company and position for the person. An effective tool for this at IBM has been behavioral-based structured interviews.

As crucial as talent selection is, it is only the beginning. Employee orientation and onboarding are critical not only to employee productivity, but also to employee retention. Onboarding, especially when seen as a long-term process, determines in large part whether new employees find their places, begin to make contributions quickly, and discover paths for growth that makes them choose long-term involvement. Talent selection and successful onboarding are the linchpins of career development and employee engagement. They set the stage for everything else that follows.

Endnotes

[1]Guthridge, Matthew; Komm, Asmus B.; Lawson, Emily. "Making talent a strategic priority," *McKinsey Quarterly*, January 2008. p. 2. More than 10,000 respondents completed the 2006 survey. The 2007 survey on organization was completed by more than 1,300 executives.

[2]Sincavage, Jessica R. "The labor force and unemployment: three generations of change," *Monthly Labor Review*, United States Bureau of Labor Statistics. June 2004. p. 36.

[3]United States Department of Labor, Bureau of Labor Statistics. News. USDL 07-1847. Employment Projections: 2006-2016. December 14, 2007. pp. 1-2.

[4]Sincavage, Jessica R. June 2004. op. cit. p. 36.

[5]Generation Y. Wikipedia, http://en.wikipedia.org/wiki/Generation_Y#Howe_and_Strauss:_.22The_Millenials.22.

[6]Guthridge, Matthew; Komm, Asmus B.; Lawson, Emily. January 2008. op. cit. p. 4.

[7]Kaiser Associates, Inc., "Making On-boarding Work: Driving Organizational Effectiveness through Improved New Hire Retention, Quicker Time-to-Productivity, Accelerated Career Advancement & Enhanced Recruitment Results," http://www.KaiserAssociates.com, 2007: p. 3.

[8]Ibid, p. 4.

[9]Platz, Brian. "Employee Onboarding: One Chance for a Positive New Employee Experience," About.com http://humanresources.about.com/od/orientation/a/onboarding.htm.

[10]Kaiser Associates, Inc. 2007. loc. cit. p. 4.

[11]IBM 2008 Annual Report. "Generating Higher Value at IBM," p. 2, ftp://ftp.software.ibm.com/annualreport/2008/2008_ibm_higher_value.pdf.

[12]IBM 2008 Annual Report. "Management Discussion: Employees and Related Workforce," p. 1, http://www.ibm.com/annualreport/2008/md_7erw.shtml.

[13]IBM 2008 Annual Report. loc. Cit. p. 1.

[14]Friedman, Laurie. "Are You Losing Potential New Hires at Hello?" *T+D* magazine, November, 2006: p. 25.

[15]IBM Human Resources Team. IBM Intranet. Employment—External Hiring Website.

[16]Hansen, Katharine, Ph.D. "Quintessential Careers™: Behavioral Interviewing Strategies for Job Seekers," http://www.quintcareers.com/behavioral_interviewing.html.

[17]Pass, John; Delany, Tanya; Thurston, Chuck. "Interviewing: IBM's Behavioral Based Structured Approach: Steps," *Manager QuickView*. Modified March 31, 2006.

[18]IBM Human Resources Team. *IBM Behavioral Based Structured Interview Reference Guide*. p. 4.

[19]Bopp, Mary Ann; Wasson, Maura. "Rapid Acclimation: IBM's Innovative Approach to Training New Employees" presentation. May 9, 2006. p. 8.

[20]Cochran, Barbara Ann. Hire Touch Group. "New Employee Orientation Programs: The Key to Starting Employees Off Right," http://www.babyshopmagazine.com/spring00/employee.htm.

[21]Taylor, Craig R. "The Tides of Talent," *T+D*, April, 2003. pp. 34–38.

[22]Kroth, Michael. *The Manager as Motivator* (Westport, CT; Greenwood Press, Praeger Publishers, 2006), Chapter 1.

[23]Kirkpatrick, D.L. *Evaluating Training Programs: The Four Levels* (San Francisco, CA: Berrett-Koehler, 1994).

[24]Your IBM Team. "IBM: New Employee Learning Program. Impact Measurement Results," October 2005.

[25]Cannon, Michael. "New Employee Experience, Effectiveness, and Success." IBM Corporation, April 8, 2009.

[26]Ibid.

[27]Ibid.

[28]Ibid.

Chapter 5 Contents

5

Assessing Levels of Expertise and Taking Action to Drive Business Success

General Overview

Numerous companies across the globe have come to realize that there is a shortage of talent and skills in their industry and even closer to home, in their companies. Despite this stark reality, many companies are ill-prepared to rectify this issue, which has the potential to adversely impact their revenue streams. "Bridging the Skills Gap," an article written by American Society of Training and Development (ASTD), Public Policy Council in the fall of 2006, reinforced this concept by noting that "Too many workers lack the right skills to help their employers grow and succeed." The article goes on to say, "At the same time that the global, knowledge-based economy places an ever-growing premium on the talent, creativity, and efficiency of the workforce, business leaders talk of the widening gap between the skills their organizations need to grow the current capabilities of their employees."[1]

Prudent and business-savvy companies need to be cognizant of their bench strength for both short-term and anticipated long-term needs. This begins with an understanding of the nature, quantity, and depth of their employees' expertise, which enables the organization to quickly identify experts who can move the organization forward by delivering rapid solutions to clients.

The inclusion of expertise requirements in business plans and forecasting is critical to the success of any company. An organization's expertise portfolio and talent management should be under constant evaluation to determine whether or not the company is poised to meet client needs, market demands, and market volatility. This expertise portfolio encompasses a diversity of requisite skills, subject matter knowledge, and personal attributes such as leadership competencies and characteristics that are essential for near- and long-term deployment when and where necessary. The keen attention that an organization pays to its expertise portfolio puts it in a ready mode to deliver solutions and services to its clients and enables it to win in the marketplace.

Expertise assessment is the process an organization uses to compare the current skill and competency levels to the tactical and strategic needs of the business and is a critical element in managing talent, particularly in multinational companies. Factors such as demographic changes, cultural differences, learning preferences and styles, as well as the diversity of needs and state-of-the-art learning tools all have an impact on a company's expertise management. These factors should be given much consideration when developing expertise assessments and business projections. These factors dictate that leaders who are responsible for the management of expertise must have the foresight to move away from the traditional "one–size-fits-all" approach in deploying learning options and resources, to a simple but blended and flexible approach to learning.

To put IBM's expertise management approach in context; it becomes necessary to know how the company defines the term. IBM defines expertise as "the sum of indicators of proven ability and experience which includes IBM competencies, functional and technical skills and subject knowledge."[2] As we progress further into the chapter, the term "expertise" will refer to this meaning.

In short, these are some of the compelling reasons why IBM makes it a practice to constantly assess, refresh, and revitalize its employees' learning practices, using practical and flexible approaches in delivering learning to its global workforce. This chapter focuses on the importance of expertise forecasting and assessment as one of the first critical tasks required to build individual employee and organizational capability and emphasizes the importance of linking business strategy with expertise development and learning needs. Also it provides a view of how IBM approaches expertise assessment. The intent is to develop and maintain a robust portfolio of the right expertise that enables IBM to respond quickly to the needs of its global clients.

Assessing the Organization's Expertise Portfolio–An Ongoing Business Necessity

A normal business practice of assessing levels of expertise helps organizations better anticipate and plan for unforeseen marketplace needs, rather than being surprised by them. Identifying skill and competency gaps in a timely manner enables the company to rapidly and creatively design plans that can bridge those gaps. Using this approach helps companies become agile in response to their clients and remain strong contenders in the global marketplace.

In order to improve the employee experience, as expertise assessments are done, consideration must be given to an array of learning options, such as tools and techniques that increase the speed of learning, overall expertise management, personalized career guidance, and creation of an atmosphere where collaborative learning is commonplace. IBM's approach to assessing organizational learning is predicated on an integrative, blended, and work-embedded process that takes into consideration the variety of employee needs and interests. It is critical to the assessment process that the company not only defines which skills are important to the business for the near- and long-term, but also to ensure there is clear understanding of the demand for and supply of such skills. This process includes the mapping of an external talent recruiting strategy, which is balanced with an internal skills and talent development plan to identify specific gaps, as well as the magnitude of the challenge that the organization faces in resolving these skill gap issues. Typically, a skill gap is the comparison of the current and projected future supply of talent that will position the organization to deliver solutions and services to the marketplace in a quality and timely manner. Once skill gaps are determined, a necessary next step is to do a thorough analysis of the nature of these gaps. The analysis ensures that the necessary training, systems, tools, and support are in place to rapidly close the identified gaps. A plan to help employees gain the required skills in a timely manner is included in the analysis, thus improving employee performance and contribution to the organization. This process requires a certain amount of rigor that should help the organization answer the following questions during the expertise assessment phase:

- Which employees possess the required skills?
- What other employees demonstrate the aptitude and baseline knowledge to quickly master these required skills?
- Will the current skills be adequate to address the needs?
- If not, what measures must be taken to close skill gaps?
- Will the company's actions include external recruiting for new talent to the business?
- Will the company's actions include a blended approach, such as formal training, the use of technology to deliver the training, experiential learning such as mentoring, job shadowing, or other means to close skills gaps?
- What are the implications to the business if such gaps are not closed?

Constant market analysis and trend analysis must be done to understand the emerging skills needs within the industry that the company serves. Parallel activities should be taking place to include skills needs—what will your company's talent and expertise profile look like in a year, five years, or even ten years? IBM Global Business Services conducted The Global Human Capital Study in 2008 and summarized its findings in the article, "Unlocking the DNA of the Adaptable Workforce." Participants in the study included more than 400 organizations that extended across 40 countries that represented a cross section of company size, industry, and geography. The study revealed that "Only 13% of the organizations interviewed believe they have clear understanding of the skills they will require in the next three to five years. While some organizations believe they understand the needs of their current businesses, they are less sure of their ability to predict the skills needed in new or emerging markets."[3]

Expertise management has become an increasingly complex exercise for many organizations, particularly those that are multinational and competing in multiple arenas, such as mature, growth, and emerging markets. All of these markets are dynamically unpredictable and very difficult to read, due to the speed of change and the demand for more sophisticated and complex skills across several geographies. Consequently, the assessment of skills within organizations has to be constant and on-going—not just the once-a-year activity to which many companies are accustomed. In his book, *Talent: Making People Your Competitive Advantage*, Edward Lawler III underscored the complex nature of skills assessment when he noted that "Acquiring the right talent is becoming an increasingly complex and challenging activity. The workforce itself has become more global, virtual, and diverse than it ever has been. Increasingly, a surplus of investment capital is chasing a scarcity of talented people. The future is more of the same; thus, organizations that excel at talent management will continue to enjoy competitive advantage."[4]

Multinational organizations must take added measures to ensure that their expertise assessment model is an integrated end-to-end process that takes into consideration varying skills needs by geographic regions. This process affords the organization the capability to deploy the right skills to the right place in the right time to respond to the needs of their global clients. Such a practice builds agility and adaptability in responding to clients anywhere and at any time.

Aligning Expertise Management with Business Strategy

The issue of expertise management will continue to require companies to find simple, affordable, and innovative ways to develop the necessary talent and capability of its workforce. As organizations create their business strategies, it is imperative that they include expertise assessment and talent development as core components of the strategy. When the business strategy is developed, there should be a built-in plan to periodically assess whether the necessary skills are being developed at the right pace and whether there are ample opportunities for employees to apply these skills in innovative ways. To stay consistent and focused on expertise management, some suggested tips and questions to determine the status of the strength of the organization's expertise portfolio are listed here:

- **Read the environment**—What is the organization's short-term/long-term strategy? Multinational organizations must look at economic trends and client requirements in the various geographic regions to determine unique needs. They need to understand what it takes to keep current customers satisfied and how to recruit new customers—executing a plan for success is contingent on having a solid workforce talent and expertise plan that drives execution and business performance.

- **Define talent posture**—Once business strategies have been defined, a skills needs analysis must be performed. The supply and demand approach should help to shape the strength and viability of the expertise portfolio of the organization. Therefore the following questions must be addressed: How many people within the organization possess the right skill sets? Are these current skills at the right level of mastery, and does the organization have adequate numbers of these skills to support the strategy? Does the organization have enough current employees who could acquire these required skills, or is it necessary to recruit externally to build the bench strength?
- **Design the solution**—The process of determining the skills that are needed and how many are available is part of the gap analysis, which was defined earlier in the chapter. The results of the expertise gap analysis must be used to drive the next necessary steps. As soon as the skills portfolio of the organization is determined, action plans must be defined to create a supply of talent for near- and long-term needs. This should include a variety of blended and integrated learning actions—that is, classroom versus e-learning and experiential learning activities.
- **Consider application and practice**—Are employees given meaningful opportunities to apply their newly acquired skills in significant ways? Do they have expert mentors to provide on-going support and guidance? Is there a plan to encourage employees to pass on their knowledge to others? As skills forecasting is taking place, are provisions being made to give employees opportunities to learn both through just-in-time means and through formal classroom training? Additionally, will the learning opportunities include tacit/experiential learning, such as shadow experience, rotational assignments, and on-the-job training? Will the organization create opportunities to help employees apply their newly acquired knowledge and expertise in meaningful ways?
- **Build in measurements**—A process must be defined to assess the speed at which skills are being developed: Are skills gaps being closed in a timely manner? Are people applying newly acquired skills? Are employees making it a practice to share and transfer critical skills to their peers? What is the overall impact?
- **Plan for the long-term**—As industry standards and client needs constantly change, organizations will realize that this will drive a possible shift in their current talent management and skills-forecasting plans. This is due primarily to the fact that changes in the industry will require a revised talent model to meet emerging business opportunities. As new

skill gaps develop, both the organization and employees must rapidly retool or enhance their skills and expertise portfolios in order to meet needs of the ever-changing marketplace. Again, expertise portfolios need to be aligned with the changing business models dictated by a marketplace that is in constant metamorphosis.

- **Build a skill bank**—A skill bank serves as a repository of the current skills profile along with the future skills that are required to help an organization respond to the needs of the marketplace. The skill bank also facilitates the design of appropriate training and development programs. Smart and proactive companies must have a repository of skills to respond to the dynamic nature of their industry and client set. Responsive companies typically are flexible and adaptable to change and are able to maintain their competitive advantage by creating "people advantage." Such an advantage is pivotal in business performance and helps companies to be proactive in assessing and mapping the learning plans of their employees.
- **Connect business plans to talent development**—The successful development of expertise and talent within an organization has to be built upon a holistic and integrated approach that aggressively creates and applies knowledge. As business strategies are developed, the company has to define up front the skills necessary to execute the strategic plans; this cannot be an afterthought. During the business strategy and forecasting phase, assessments must be made to determine the skills that are required to meet current and future business needs. This plan might include the methods that the company will use to acquire the right skills. As an example, will the company use external recruiting efforts to supply the necessary skills, or will they rely primarily on the internal development of skills? Either way, the necessary budget and funding must be in place to build the appropriate levels of expertise that the company needs to meet business plans, and all these factors must be addressed during the business planning and forecasting phase.

Figure 5.1 summarizes the various talent and expertise processes, which are intricately linked to the company's forecasting priorities and strategy. When an organization has the right levels of expertise available by making this linkage between talent/expertise planning and strategic business priorities, it is proactively focusing on all the elements that help to achieve its business goals.

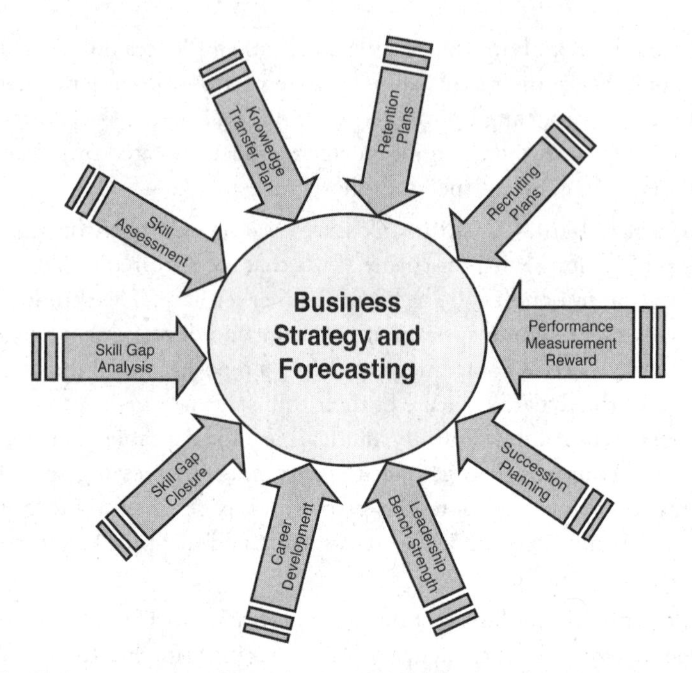

Figure 5.1 Business strategy and forecasting: a critical link to talent management.

Aligning Employee Interests and Career Aspirations with Skills Forecasting

Generally, employees derive a sense of value if their career goals and interests are important factors in a company's business strategy and skills forecasting process and when there is a clear line of sight as to how they can achieve their personal and career goals while contributing at a level commensurate with their potential. Organizations cannot overlook the importance of including stated or perceived employee career interests, personal goals, and professional aspirations when they are assessing and defining current and future skills needs. Employee career interests should be included in the forecasting process to signal to them that their growth and desire to acquire new skills are essential factors in helping to build organizational capability that translates into competitive advantage in the marketplace. When employees perceive that their interests to grow within the organization are taken seriously, it allows them to see that they are part of shaping the future success of the organization, instilling meaning and purpose both for them and for the organization.

Employees are more motivated to learn when they see how their knowledge and skills can make a difference for the organization. Inevitably, this establishes a learning culture in which people become focused on acquiring new skills, and as they do, they are energized by helping others grow.

As expertise forecasting is taking place, the leaders of the organization must be mindful of the characteristics, qualities, and personal attributes employees need to develop. These characteristics include an on-going thirst for knowledge as well as a willingness to share knowledge along with the desire to constantly seek innovative ways to apply their knowledge. The application of acquired knowledge is a key aspect of the learning process, and organizations should reinforce the importance of the learning-and-doing approach. To this point, the Society of Human Resource Management in their 2008 first quarter research paper, "A Gateway to Organizational Success," supports this learning in stating that "Another key model regarding training is the cognitive theory of transfer, a process model of learning. In training programs, training transfer is further enhanced through application assignments that create simulations to apply learning in the work setting (e.g., identification of work problems and situations), thus linking learned capability and real world application."[5] As employees' interests in learning new skills are met, the organization should create opportunities to help them transfer learning theory into meaningful practical application. Organizations must be open to the idea that mistakes will be made as employees apply their newly acquired skills, and when such mistakes occur, they must be treated as learning opportunities. The practice of treating mistakes as learning opportunities is an important way to analyze why the mistakes occurred in the first place and determine what could have been done differently. Doing a root cause analysis of organizational mistakes is essential in forestalling the recurrence of the same mistakes. Over time, if the same organizational mistakes continue to take place, it will prove to be costly to the organization.

Tools and Practices to Support the Development of Expertise

Given the high premium placed on intellectual capital, it is necessary for companies to create an environment that fosters continuous learning, intellectual stimulation, and on-going support for the development of their employees. Consistent with the business strategy, a plan must be defined to identify the necessary learning tools and resources available to employees. It is highly recommended that companies examine their current learning tools and resources to determine whether or not they are outdated. Outdated learning tools generally are unable to meet the constantly changing demands of the workplace; some of the indicators include slow response time and not having enough capacity and functionalities to facilitate the necessary learning needs in a timely manner. Organizations must also establish methods and plans for upgrading learning tools to keep abreast of the changing learning needs. Having tools with the right capabilities that simplify the learning experience for employees will make the learning experience a rewarding one. Making the available tools' user-friendly and clearly mapping out the learning process signals to the employees that their development is important to the success of the business.

As an illustration, IBM's employee development approach is to invest in making it possible for employees to acquire, develop, and apply their expertise to deliver business results, while allowing them the opportunity to advance and attain their career goals and aspirations. The IBM approach to skills acquisition and career development is predicated on a simple, integrated, "one-stop" method to learning, made possible by the enhancement of the learning tools available to employees. The step-by-step process IBM uses to develop employees takes the guesswork out of the system and thereby reinforces the importance of employee development. This simplified process promotes and accelerates the development of expertise. Here is the learning model that IBM uses in developing their employees:

- Employees have access to an expertise assessment tool that gives them a reading of their current expertise and skills and offers them recommended learning. The recommended development activities are associated with specific job roles.
- Employees are encouraged to have career discussions with their managers to review learning recommendations, determine expertise gaps, and agree on plans to bridge those gaps.
- Employees include their development goals and plans for skill gap closure in their career development plan. The plan should be reviewed by the employee's immediate managers in order to gain agreement on the

developmental needs and the plans to address those needs. The development plan should be a live document that is reviewed periodically to ensure that progress is being made to close skill gaps.

- Employees are encouraged to share their plans with their mentors to enlist additional support. Mentors play a critical role in helping their mentees close skill gaps.
- Employees are encouraged to close skill gaps for their current jobs, as well as developing skills for future roles within IBM.
- Employees are required to develop expertise in multiple areas across the business and not limit themselves to acquiring skills for their current jobs. This includes developing technical and functional skills, as well as global leadership skills and business acumen. This ultimately leads to growth in both individual employee and organizational capability.

To fully engage them in the learning process, IBM tells employees why skills assessment is important in achieving their career goals and shows them how to increase their value to the business. The learning plans that employees receive are tailored to their specific growth needs. While this process allows employees to take responsibility for their development, managers also play a pivotal role in partnering with and supporting employees in the learning and development process. The ultimate goal is to provide employees with the necessary tools, support, and clarity regarding performance expectations. As employees develop new expertise, the expectation is that they will perform and increase their value proposition to the business.

The employee development process holds managers responsible for identifying new leaders within their departments in order to create organization succession plans. This exercise is forward-thinking and positions IBM to develop a pool of future leaders so that easy and smooth transitions can be made.

Employee Succession Planning–Strategically Important to the Business

Succession planning is a vitally important process that consists of the development of leaders who have the necessary skills, attributes, and depth to execute important business ventures across a global market. As companies make projections for the future, building organizational capabilities is high on the list. Equally important is the need to continually renew the diverse pool of new leaders. Succession planning generally focuses on highly visible leadership positions that are of critical importance to the business. Positions such as this play a role in shaping the current and future success of the business, and when staffing changes occur in these positions, replacements must be made thoughtfully and quickly. Making rapid replacement decisions results in minimal disruption to internal operations and will be seamless to customers. The January 2008 McKinsey Quarterly, *Making Talent a Strategic Priority*, noted that "Our experience during the past decade shows that companies must do much more to ensure their access to a sufficient supply of talented people. Demographics, globalization and the characteristics of knowledge work present long-term challenges that reinforce the argument for putting workforce planning and talent management at the heart of business strategy and for giving those issues a bigger share of senior management's time."[6]

A systematic approach in succession planning should be taken, one in which the organization has a blueprint that identifies new potential leaders on a continual basis. As these future leaders are identified, they should immediately have mentors and role models available to them to speed up their development. In 2002 Pepperdine University Graziadio Business School published an article, "Choose Tomorrow's Leaders Today," which reported that best practice companies like Sonoco, Dow, and Dell, to name a few, focus on "monitoring future needs, talent assessments, use of technology to integrate data, developmental activities, and performance measurements as key components of their succession planning best practice methods." The report cited that "Dow has moved from having different competencies for each global business to a common set of seven used throughout the corporation. Dell focuses on a "global corporate talent," which consists of individuals who have the capability to "run significant portions of a...business...on a global basis. They also track functional high potentials."[7]

Given the complexities, ambiguities, volatility, and dynamic nature of the twenty-first century global workplace, the need for new leadership competencies has never been higher. Companies such as IBM are investing heavily in developing current and future leaders to master such qualities as

- Depth and breadth in technical and global business knowledge

- A record of excellence and being known as true thought leaders in their areas of expertise
- The ability to tackle difficult problems head-on and knowing when to seek input and guidance from others
- Being a natural visionary who is not intimidated by taking calculated and informed risks
- The ability to see the big picture without losing sight of the small but important things
- The ability to deliver rapid results and value to global clients
- The ability to inspire self and others—"light the fire in people instead of under people"
- Instilling a sense of meaning and purpose in others
- The ability to lead, motivate, and develop others

As part of the succession planning process, future leaders must be given the opportunity to acquire a versatile set of experiences across the organization and not be limited to gaining experience only within one organization. IBM makes it a practice to create opportunities for employees to develop broad cross-organizational leadership and business experience throughout the company. Thus, it stands to reason that programs such as rotational, temporary, and global assignments are essential to the development of new leaders within IBM. Career development and succession planning are critical components of a thriving business. Every effort should be made to identify those difficult-to-replace employees who have knowledge that is essential to the business, and furthermore a strong retention and engagement plan must also be implemented.

The investment in succession planning helps the organization to "construct a leadership, knowledge and experience repertoire," which can be used as an organizational arsenal against competitors in the marketplace. David W. DeLong, in his book *Lost Knowledge*, reinforces the importance of putting in place a retention plan that compliments succession planning. To this point, DeLong states that "While succession planning can help preempt knowledge loss for the organization, career development processes may be one of the most effective retention tools for key employees. Career development processes can increase retention in the tight labor markets by signaling to individuals that the organization is interested in their personal development."[8]

Critical to the issue of succession planning is the challenge that companies face regarding the aging of the workforce and the imminent loss of intellectual and human capital through the retirement of Baby Boomers. The attention that is given to the development of an organization's leadership and knowledge bench strength is consuming the time of many Human Resources organizations across the globe. It is in this perspective that the notion of "leaders building leaders" has become an expectation in IBM, and it is part of the robust knowledge transfer system that has helped to stem the impact of retiring Baby Boomers. In short, Robert Gandossy and Marc Effron in their book *Leading the Way*, reported that during the Gerstner era, "A comprehensive approach to building great leaders was crafted, including careful selection, development, and rewards for IBM's best talent. Leaders were held accountable for growing other leaders, and good leadership was viewed as a critical asset to be carefully managed for the best possible return."[9] Current leaders are expected to play an integral role in the development process of the generation of leaders that are behind them. Sharing their experiences, which include career setbacks, recovery from setbacks, career choices, career decisions, and successes, are important topics to discuss in helping to develop new leaders.

Changing Workforce Demographics–A Factor to Be Assessed

With the changing demographics of the workplace, companies are grappling with the issue of creating an environment that supports collaborative learning and the critical requirement of transferring knowledge as Baby Boomers retire. These issues also come into play as companies retrench their workforces when economic times turn sour and resources leave the company—voluntarily or involuntarily. When adverse business conditions begin to turn around, companies might find they no longer have the key skills required to grow again. To create this learning environment, companies must address the varying needs of each generation that is present in the workplace. For the purpose of clarity and consistency, as noted in Chapter 4, "Selecting the Best Talent and Developing New Employees," individuals born between 1946 and 1964 are considered the Baby Boomer generation, and Gen X and Gen Y were born between 1965 and 1975 and 1976 and 2001, respectively.

The twenty-first century has heralded a number of challenges that are germane to the changing demographics of the workforce, and many organizations are strugling to address these challenges. Organizations that do not make an earnest effort to put plans in place to address the imminent impact of demographic changes will experience severe difficulty retaining the collective knowledge of those leaving the company. Furthermore, organizations that fail to plan for demographic changes will be caught flat-footed when it comes to developing a variety of learning options for today's workforce, that is made up of multiple generations. This issue becomes complicated because each generation has a different set of skills needs, coupled with varying career development expectations from the organization.

To underscore the challenges of the demographic changes that organizations face, The IBM Global Business Services, in partnership with the American Society for Training and Development (ASTD), coauthored an article that speaks to the "shifting workforce demographics and the learning function." The article stated that "Changing workforce demographics are having a notable effect on organizations across a variety of industries and geographies. While the learning function has significant opportunities to help companies address issues associated with this shift, it needs to reorient its focus and capabilities. To help mitigate the challenges of retiring workers and their subsequent replacements, the learning function needs to play a role in areas such as determining critical skills and capabilities, transferring knowledge and reducing time-to-competence for newer employees."[10]

We previously noted that skills forecasting has to be aligned with business forecasting and assessments in order to build the talent base and the intellectual capital of the organization. Interestingly, forecasting must also encompass the demographic trends of the workforce, including a direct link to the diversity and inclusion strategies of the organization.

As an illustration, the organization must have a sense not only of who might leave the business through retirement, but also the concomitant impact of the intellectual capital that would also be exiting the business. There has been much discussion about the fact that due to the large numbers of Baby Boomers who will soon be eligible to retire, companies are going to incur a severe knowledge and expertise drain. Unfortunately, however, many organizations are having difficulty to harness and transfer that knowledge quickly enough to avoid an adverse impact on the business. In essence, the organizational plans to "pass on the torch of knowledge and experience" to the generation behind must be a priority in the assessment and strategy planning phase of the organization. The alignment of skills and talent strategies to diversity strategies is an essential process in the quest to capture organizational knowledge. This is due primarily to the critical need to bridge generational differences and conflicts that typically occur when the four distinct generational groups work together.

These differences may originate from the contrasting styles and approaches to doing work or from the perception that what a new Gen X or Gen Y hire values may be totally different from what a Baby Boomer values. There are also differences from generation to generation in the way that decisions are made, career needs and aspirations are met, excitement and fun are generated, and purpose is created. Through diversity education and awareness, it is possible to move the generations from conflict to collaboration, and once collaboration is achieved, it then creates and fosters a healthy climate where knowledge transfer becomes a focus of the generational groups.

Lynne C. Lancaster and David Stillman, in their book, *When Generations Collide*, reinforced the point that "In general the generations tend to have a pretty narrow bandwidth of tolerance for one another. We give our peers much more leeway than we give someone from another generation." To create meaningful learning opportunities, fun and excitement must be a part of the process. To this point, Lancaster and Stillman add that "Fun deepens the learning and deepens the bonds, especially among people of different generations who might normally never encounter each other on that level."[11]

To overcome the generational divide and bring cultural understanding, learning events and functions must elucidate topics related to workplace demographics and other diversity dimensions. Once these gaps are closed, it influences the opportunity for employees to learn together and to collaborate in more meaningful and productive ways. If this can be achieved, a climate of collaborative learning ensues, and the easy flow of knowledge and information is transmitted among the generations that are present in the workplace. This level of skills assessment and creating learning tools to address these issues makes it relatively easy to "pass on the torch of experience."

Varying Approaches to Managing Talent and Skills to Build the Enterprise of the Future–What Drives IBM?

In 2008, IBM conducted its third biennial Global CEO Study with more than 1,000 participants from both the public and private sectors. One of the cornerstones of the study was to focus on the "Enterprise of the Future," in which there is a demand to integrate capabilities globally to differentiate the organization of the past from the one that is being designed for the future. The Enterprise of the Future searches worldwide for sources of expertise, resources, and assets that can be easily and readily deployed to deliver service and solutions. "Finding the right capabilities is much more important than finding the cheapest ones. These centers of excellence are integrated globally so that the best capabilities, knowledge and assets can be used wherever required."[12] As a practice, IBM makes it a priority to constantly assess the skills and capabilities of its global workforce and uses this information to refresh, identify, and catalog the portfolio of expertise and talent that exists within the company. The intent is to be able to unleash this portfolio of skills anywhere in the enterprise whenever it is needed and at a moment's notice.

IBM has a longstanding history of developing its people with the right skills, not just for the moment or for the current job, but for the future success of the business. As early as 1961, T.J. Watson, Jr. asserted that "IBM's future is in the hands of its people. Our future is unlimited."[13]

The development of talent continues to be of utmost importance to IBM, and employees are given resources and support to develop a diverse set of skills that are not only relevant to their development, but are also relevant to the company's growth and success. The skills that employees possess represent specialization and depth along with broad knowledge in other important, related areas. At the same time, these employees are given the opportunity to apply both the specialized and broad skills that can help the business deliver integrated solutions to its global clients. A basic tenet of IBM's concept of the Globally Integrated Enterprise is that the company is making it a business necessity to develop a supply of high-value talent and expertise that can be located anywhere in the enterprise. This approach has created renewed excitement about skills development and the desire for continuous learning, and if it becomes necessary, employees are willing to re-invent and re-tool their skills portfolio. Employees realize that the business benefits by helping them retool their skills to align with the company's strategy of reinventing the way business is done in order to meet changing marketplace demands. To substantiate the importance of investing in employee development, IBM defined its learning strategy, which articulates how its people can play a role in the future success of the business. The IBM Learning Strategy clearly states that "Our people are a critical factor to achieving long-term profitable growth. Supporting our learning strategy is an investment in the future of IBM. The Learning function's role is to help our company learn, adopt, adapt and grow."[14]

Incubating Talent for Business Success–The IBM Way

To cultivate new talent and build on what already exists within the organization, IBM developed an integrated expertise management system that brought all the disparate and disjointed learning components into a streamlined, one-stop-shop portfolio of learning options. The structure of the expertise management system is adaptable and flexible, and the primary intent is to ensure that adjustments can be easily made according to country and geographic regions. IBM is in a never-ending mode of assessing skills needs and finding ways to effectively manage global talent, and thus the prediction and assessment of skills remain a priority for the company. The assessment is carried out in a rapid manner in order to meet the needs not only of the mature markets, but even more importantly in the emerging markets, where talent is typically scarce. The IBM expertise model is constructed on speed to recruit the right skills into the business and speed to help current employees acquire, master, and apply critical skills in ways that help IBM to remain relevant in a competitive global marketplace. According to Frank Persico, IBM Vice President, Workforce Learning and Development, "Having built a complete suite of enduring capabilities for Learning Leadership, Expertise Management and the provision of Personalized Learning and Career Guidance, we are now positioned to deliver significantly higher levels of business value to IBM."[15]

The IBM Expertise Management System is aligned very closely to its career framework, and this connection begins with the definition of a common and consistent "taxonomy" for job roles and skills all across IBM. This process introduces a high degree of clarity to the IBM workforce, which has resulted in enabling employees to take a more active role in identifying and articulating the expertise and skills they need to develop in their current jobs. In addition, with this understanding, employees are equipped with the knowledge of how to do their skills and competency mapping to meet their future career goals and aspirations. Personal career guidance is given to employees to help them balance their current skill set with the skills they will need to fulfill future job roles. Employees find this process empowering because it gives them the tools and resources to act responsibly about their development and helps them better engage in more substantive and higher quality career discussions with their managers and mentors.

Removing the Mystery from Career Development–IBM Defines a Holistic Approach

The IBM Expertise Management system is a centralized career development hub that offers employees across the enterprise recommendations on options and tools to assess their skills. Employees are also given learning recommendations that are relevant to their unique needs. IBM paid particular attention to designing a career development program that is integrated and links all the relevant components of the learning process. This approach has notably improved the employee learning experience and in essence encourages expertise and talent development across the business. Because all the learning components are integrated and it is easy to use, employees are taking charge of their own development with the support of their managers.

Here are some of the learning components connected to the Expertise Management process:

- **Learning website**—Recommends learning activities and career guidance to help employees to develop their capabilities.
- **Career website**—Focuses on a variety of ways employees can develop their careers.
- **Competencies**—Includes competencies that are leveraged as part of the performance evaluation process by demonstrating how employees distinguish themselves in the way they perform their jobs.
- **New employee onboarding**—Addresses ways to quickly introduce new hires to IBM by exposing them to the IBM values, provide them with the appropriate support system, and help them understand the opportunities and growth potential that are available to them.

- **Workforce Management Initiative**—Integrates, anticipates, and forecasts current and future skills needs and gives IBM a comprehensive view of the capabilities and expertise that exist across the enterprise.

The IBM workforce is characterized as high performing and highly skilled. The company maintains this posture by developing detailed career models and is vigilant in adjusting these models based on changing marketplace demands, simplifying learning processes, and providing employees with clarity on ways to achieve their career aspirations. The *McKinsey Quarterly* January 2008: "Making Talent a Strategic Priority" cites that "Companies like to promote the idea that employees are their biggest source of competitive advantage. Yet the astonishing reality is that most of them are as unprepared for the challenge of finding, motivating and retaining capable workers as they were a decade ago."[16]

IBM has a history of reinventing itself according to the dynamic and volatile nature of the clients they serve. As the company reinvents itself, it has to quickly assess the skills that are required to support the success of the new business structure because IBM understands that investing in talent development is an on-going priority that is aligned with business strategy. IBM realizes that its intellectual and expertise bench strength are predictors of how it competes in the global marketplace. People are IBM's future and IBM's success. In 1974, the CEO of IBM endorsed the value IBM places in its people by asserting that "Our investment in education is large, and the reason is plain: We cannot hope to run the IBM of tomorrow on yesterday's knowledge. It is vital for each of us to keep abreast of new knowledge, whatever our job."[17] The enduring skills that IBM has enabled its workforce to develop have been a key factor in helping the company to maintain its brand as an "employer of choice" and a "solution provider of choice." Developing its people has been a historical practice for IBM; the only change in this regard is that a more dedicated focus has been given to better integrating skills assessments and forecasting in the overall business model and strategy planning. In addition, the process for development is streamlined, the approach is holistic, and employees are given tools to do their own skills assessments. As employees acquire new skills, they are held accountable to improve performance and add value to the business.

Summary

In summary, this chapter highlights the importance of aligning business forecasting and strategy development with skills forecasting and on-going assessments. Failing to make skills assessment a critical aspect of a company's business strategy can result in skills and talent deficiencies that can impede an organization's ability to deliver quality services and solutions to its clients in a timely manner. IBM has made skills assessment a priority, and it has yielded a record of success in the global marketplace. IBM's principal focus is to optimize the skills and capabilities of its workforce in order to become more adaptable to the fickle and sometimes unpredictable nature of the global marketplace. IBM states that "In order to do this, we must transform three elements: reinvent management processes, provide relevant and timely learning for employees, and reduce cultural barriers to change. The result is an end-to-end workforce management solution to improve IBM's efforts to help clients succeed and drive greater innovation across the enterprise."[18] It is obvious that IBM not only recognizes that developing its people is the right thing to do, but it also recognizes that it is essential in driving sustained business success.

Endnotes

[1]ASTD Public Policy Council. "Bridging the Skills Gap: How the Skills Shortage Threatens Growth and Competitiveness and What To Do About It," Fall 2006.

[2]IBM. "WMI Glossary"—Expertise Management homepage reference section, 2006.

[3]Ringo, Tom, IBM Global Business Services, and Randy MacDonald, Senior VP HR, IBM, "Unlocking the DNA of the Adaptable Workforce—The Global Human Capital Study 2008."

[4]Lawler, Edward E., III. *Talent: Making People Your Competitive Advantage* (San Francisco: Jossey-Bass, 2008).

[5]Noe, R.A. 2008 First Quarter Research—SHRM. "Strategic Training and Development: A Gateway to Organizational Success," March 2008. Quote taken from Employee Training and Development, 3rd edition, 2005.

[6]Guthridge, Matthew, Asmus B. Komm, and Emily Lawson. "Making Talent a Strategic Priority," *The McKinsey Quarterly*: January 2008.

[7]Fulmer, Robert M., Ph.D. "Choose Tomorrow's Leader Today: Succession Planning Grooms Firms for Success," Pepperdine University Graziadio Business School—Business Report, 2002, Volume 5, Issue 1.

[8]DeLong, David W. *Lost Knowledge—Confronting the Threat of an Aging Workforce* (New York: Oxford University Press, Inc., 2002) p. 66.

[9]Gandossy, Robert and Marc Effron. *Leading the Way: Three Truths from the Top Companies for Leaders* (Hoboken: John Wiley & Sons, Inc., 2004) p. 2.

[10]Lesser, Eric, Human Capital Management, IBM, and Ray Rivera, ASTD. "Closing the Generational Divide: Shifting Workforce Demographics and the Learning Function." IBM Global Business Services, in association with ASTD, 2006, p. 1.

[11]Lancaster, Lynne and David Stillman. *When Generations Collide: Who They Are. Why They Clash. How to Solve the Generational Puzzle* (New York: HarperCollins, 2002) p. 145.

[12]IBM Corporation. "The Enterprise of the Future, Implications for the Workforce" *Global CEO Study*. IBM Global Business Services, last updated October 8, 2008, p. 42.

[13]Watson, T.J., Jr. "Quintessential Quotes," The IBM Corporate Archives, 1961, p. 6.

[14]IBM Expertise Management. "Learning Strategy," June 2008, p. 1.

[15]Persico, Frank, Vice President, Workforce Learning and Development Executive. Expertise Management Home Page, June 2008.

[16]Guthridge, Matthew, Asmus B. Komm and Emily Lawson, "Making Talent a Strategic Priority," *The McKinsey Quarterly*, January 2008.

[17]Carey, Frank T., IBM Corporate Archives, 1974, p. 10.

[18]Sader, Melissa, IT Communications, and Barbara Sinopoli. "Workforce Management Initiative, Harnessing IBM's Skills and Talent: Workforce Management Supporting the On Demand Business Strategy," White Paper, updated December 2005.

Chapter 6 Contents

6

Building Employee and Organizational Capability

Changing Dynamics and Its Impact on Growing Capability

Building both organizational and employee capability will be of paramount importance for decades to come. Organizations need to deal with the many challenges caused by rapidly changing technology, the onslaught of exiting Baby Boomers, and the generational differences from the new type of workers who will be replacing them. The unprecedented financial downturn that began in 2008 will compound the problems facing an organization's ability to build capability as companies downsize and restructure their operations. Reaction to market downturn will displace some employees, particularly those in maturing economies, but will create opportunities for those who remain within the organization.

Expanding work beyond country borders is also creating challenges and opportunities. Mercer Human Resource Consulting says, "The globalization of the labor market has brought a new core competency to the table—the ability to work comfortably across languages, cultures, and time zones. People with these skills will be in great demand and will expect different career paths than what many organizations are accustomed to providing."[1]

These changes have contributed to a shorter lifespan for the skills needed in organizations and an increased need for global integration. Through interviews with 1,130 CEOs, general managers, and senior public sector and business leaders worldwide in 40 countries, the 2008 IBM Global CEO Study reveals that while CEOs are anticipating becoming more globally integrated, managing talent worldwide will be a key dependency on how effectively their organizations can achieve such goals. CEOs are focused on making changes to take advantage of global integration in a variety of ways, including entering new markets, expanding their brands and products, and optimizing their operations on a more global scale. The most prominent change cited, however, is that "57 percent of CEOs intend to change their mix of skills, capabilities, and knowledge assets around the globe."[2] The IBM Global CEO Study also says that senior HR executives are concerned about finding new talent pools and updating employee skills.[3]

Companies need to understand how all these changes impact their ability to build and retain organizational capability. It will become increasingly important for companies to focus on ensuring that employees grow their skills in order to meet new challenges that the organization may face as the economy recovers and new business models emerge.

According to an article written by Mike Brennan and Andrew Gebavi in the March 2008 issue of *Chief Learning Officer Magazine*, a survey conducted by NYU's School of Continuing and Professional Studies in 2006 showed that New York professionals of today expect to change careers more often than workers of prior generations. The idea of a lifelong career is a fading reality for a variety of reasons including a lack of defined pension plans, longer life spans, and technologies that allow employees to be more self-directed in their career exploration. It, therefore, becomes necessary for organizations to provide a flexible work environment where employees can make informed decisions to manage their careers.[4]

Companies that make the most of their global workforce take a holistic approach to managing their talent. They start with a comprehensive understanding of existing workforce demographics and capabilities and develop the ability to evaluate the current and future supply and demand for critical positions. Further, they are able to target their recruiting efforts to fill existing and potential future gaps for key job families, as well as create formal and informal development opportunities for employees whom the organization would like to retain. Global organizations that focus on talent management also apply tools and processes to connect individuals and locate expertise worldwide. Surrounding all of these efforts is an overall performance management system that is designed to provide employees with clear direction and the feedback necessary to improve their performance.[5]

To respond to these changing dynamics, organizations need to create agile career development processes that are flexible enough to build deep organizational capability. They also need to provide careers for employees in a way that builds individual capability. We now discuss how to develop organizational and individual capability by enabling employees to achieve meaningful careers that support the company in achieving its goal.

Building Careers

The key to building organizational capability begins with building individual employee capability. Employees need to focus on growing existing skills, as well as on learning new ones. They also need to gain the appropriate experiences that can help them grow their individual capabilities to match those needed by the organization to serve clients or customers. They need to understand emerging job roles and what skills are required to fill those roles—and ensure they take appropriate action to progress in their careers. They need to take even more responsibility for their own career development and managing their careers based on both the needs of the organization and their own personal aspirations. The combination of these factors will force organizations and their employees to collaborate on balancing what the company needs from its employees with what employees want from their careers.

This requires providing the appropriate structure, tools, resources, and support for employees to progress in their careers. In Chapter 3, "Defining the Career Development Process," Figure 3.1 depicts the three elements that contributed to building meaningful careers: personal goals and aspirations; company business strategy and goals; and career opportunities in the company. At the core of these elements is the partnership that needs to be forged between the organization, the manager, and the employee. We now explore how these three elements work in tandem to provide the basis for career paths that lead to building both employee, and ultimately organizational capability. In Chapter 7,

"Creating Meaningful Development Plans," we explore the importance of the partnership among the organization, the manager, and the employee in the career development process.

Considering Employee Needs When Creating Meaningful Careers

Career paths of tomorrow have begun to take different shapes than the career paths of yesterday. This can be seen today by looking at the differences in how the Generation X or Y individuals view work versus their predecessors, the Baby Boomers. In recent years, loyalty to any particular company has become a thing of the past, and today's young worker has different needs than the worker of yesterday. For instance, according to the Selection Forecast 2006–2007 cosponsored by Development Dimensions International (DDI) and Monster, responses from over 5,600 staffing directors, hiring managers, and job seekers in five global regions reveal that young employees want a fun place to work with social networks, whereas older employees moved up the ladder in a particular career and often stayed with the same company for their entire career. Employers need to be aware of these differences in order to attract younger employees' interest.[6]

Thus, companies need to understand the needs of their younger emerging workforce and craft career paths that energize such workers, rather than offer them no option but to leave prematurely.

At IBM, its Expertise Management System and career framework, first introduced in Chapter 2, "Enabling Career Advancement," provide the infrastructure that shapes career paths for IBM employees. Career paths are flexible enough to meet both personal and corporate goals as workforce needs change. The next section provides a view of IBM's approach to building careers that is enabled through its agile career development process. We begin with a description of how job roles and associated career paths are defined within the company and form the basis of the Expertise Management System. We then describe how IBM's career framework will provide an avenue for people to advance in their career over time.

Flexible Career Paths as an Essential Element of Career Development

As a company defines and changes its strategy, it is important to define and update the types of job roles and associated skills that are required in order to build organizational capability to achieve organizational goals. Employees need a guide for how they acquire the appropriate training and experiences required to progress in their careers while keeping up with these changing demands. This type of guide is often referred to as a career path or a map.

According to BNET Business Dictionary, the business definition of a career path is "a planned, logical progression of jobs within one or more professions throughout working life. A career path can be planned with greater assurance in market conditions of stability and little change."[7] However, in times where market conditions falter and layoffs are inevitable, employees need to stay abreast of their options based on the skills they possess. Whether employees are indeed laid off or whether they are among those who remain within the organization, they need to be flexible. They may need to be prepared to change "gears." What was a thriving career yesterday could diminish or even vanish tomorrow as jobs are sourced in emerging countries where labor costs are lower, or technologies change and certain job roles become obsolete.

Employees also need to continually re-assess where they are in their personal career journeys. What they need and desire at the age of 22 may be different at the age of 30 or 40 or beyond. An agile career development process can also help employees manage their careers through both good and turbulent times. The process should include guidance to employees and managers on how to develop meaningful career paths. A career path enables employees to advance in ways that are meaningful to them personally. It also provides a structure for the organization to show employees how they can acquire different skills, gain valuable experiences within one job role or through various job roles, and build capabilities that provide value to clients. While employees need to take responsibility for owning their own career paths, managers also play an integral role in helping employees plan their career paths based on employee desires and what the organization needs from its employees.

The Generalist Versus the Versatilist

If the 1980s was the era of the generalist, and the 1990s was the era of the specialist, then we are now in the era of the versatilist. In today's business arena, technical aptitude (or any single specialty) alone may not always be sufficient. "Versatilist" is the term used to describe people whose widening portfolios of roles, knowledge, insight, context, and experiences can be applied and recombined in numerous ways to fuel innovative business value. According to Wikipedia.com, "A versatilist is someone who can be a specialist for a particular discipline, while at the same time be able to change to [or perform] another role with the same ease."[8]

Employees need to be more versatile in what they know in order to compete for jobs and to remain resilient in an environment where technology and advancements in products and services change at lightning speed.

Career paths can take either a traditional approach or a versatile approach. In Chapter 2, we introduced the concept of multiple career paths. To further expand upon those concepts, on the traditional path, employees move forward by moving upward, gaining responsibility and authority in a single field. At IBM, many job categories offer focused paths for an employee's career in a particular area of specialty. Employees may spend their entire careers in one particular primary job category, such as a project manager or a consultant. They progress up the career ladder by having different jobs and experiences within their discipline, or they move between business units and gain exposure to other parts of the business. They build deep levels of expertise in their areas of specialty and are considered experts in this field.

In addition to the traditional path, IBM also offers a career path to meet the growing need for employees who are versatile, making lateral moves while expanding their skills in a career path that might span multiple job categories. According to an internal IBM website called "Advance your career," "Employees move from one field to another, responding to their own interests and the company's changing needs. They apply existing skills in new ways, share experience with colleagues, and broaden their competencies. Their rise through the hierarchy might seem slower, but they can reach positions with broader influence across departments and business units."[9] Versatile employees may be deep experts in multiple areas, although it may take years to acquire this level of in-depth expertise across several disciplines. In what is the more common scenario, employees are very well-rounded in multiple areas of the business but are not necessarily considered a thought leader in any one particular discipline. Employees with these types of versatile skills are becoming more popular across IBM as the complexity and global nature of the job roles increase. This situation is particularly prevalent in countries where there are large numbers of both employees and clients and where the complexity of client solutions may be greater. In contrast, many IBM employees are already versatilists, especially those in countries where there is a more limited client base and the IBM population is smaller, which requires each individual employee to perform multiple job roles in order to get the work done.

Both types of employees continue to be needed in IBM in response to client needs. The particular path that employees choose depends upon their individual needs as well as the overall needs of the company and where specific job roles are required. The company still requires employees with deep expertise in a particular discipline to solve very complex client problems. There is also an emerging need for employees who possess a wide range of capabilities so they can approach client opportunities in a more holistic manner.

A similar example is the case of a physician. Specialists are needed for very complex medical issues, where deep expertise can help quickly pinpoint a patient's diagnosis and treatment options. The specialist, such as a medical oncologist that treats cancer patients, has treated the same type of cancer many times in many patients and often has the latest state-of-the art testing equipment or access to in-depth research and advanced treatments. On the other hand, that same patient may need a primary care physician as well to treat other minor illnesses such as a sore throat or a cold, where the expense and expertise of a specialist is just not required. Internists often treat more than just the sore throat; they may also realize that the patient has a family that is susceptible to catching the illness from the patient and hence speaks to the patient about how to protect his or her family from catching a cold. The primary care physician approaches the treatment in a very holistic fashion and knows when to refer the patient to a specialist.

In addition to versatility, employees at IBM can pursue a professional/technical career path in which individuals carry out work, utilizing an area of expertise. Some employees also go on to pursue managerial job roles in which individuals carry out work through leveraging the skills and knowledge of others. In the latter case where a technical career path leads to a managerial job role, the manager often retains his technical expertise at some level of mastery, however, now also focuses on growing "people management" skills.

All of these types of career paths can lead to an executive career path, whereby individuals develop the company's long-term needs and strategies and provide leadership in executing them. But what guides employees? How do they determine the best way to progress along any particular path or even which path to choose?

The next section talks about how to define job roles as the basis for career paths. It shows how IBM creates flexible career paths that meet employee expectations and help achieve company talent goals.

Defining Job Roles as the Basis for Career Paths

Employees typically begin work in a company in some "job role"—or what they'll be responsible for every day. Employees also change job roles over time, whether it's within the same organization or a new organization. Job roles are an integral part of a person's career path.

At IBM, a job role is defined as a named, integrated cluster of work responsibilities and activities that need to be performed by a single person. In many cases, a single job role constitutes most of a person's responsibilities and activities. Job roles are the levels at which skilled resources can be planned, acquired, developed, and deployed, and they need to be kept to a manageable number so that the marketplace can identify easily with all of them. According to an IBM's internal Expertise Taxonomy website, "Job roles are important because they precisely define skills and ability to perform work independently or in teams. They are the skills 'DNA'; that is, they are the fundamentals that keep the people side of the...business running."[10] With job roles, IBM has a common language for recruiting, skills development, and serving the client.

Chapter 5, "Assessing Levels of Expertise and Taking Action to Drive Business Success," provided an overview of the IBM Expertise Management System, which begins with the definition of a common and consistent taxonomy for job roles and skills all across IBM. It starts by defining primary job categories and additional secondary job categories that comprise all the job roles needed across the company. Each IBM employee is in a single job category at any point in time. This is defined by the work the employee performs and the employee's position code (a unique code used for compensation purposes and is determined based on the type of work one does and the level of responsibility for that job). Job categories are global and are composed of two groupings: the primary and secondary job category.

The primary job category characterizes broad segmentations of the type of work employees perform. These categories are wide-ranging in scope. All employees are assigned to a job category based on position code.

The secondary job category identifies more specific types of work that employees may perform and are subsets of the primary job categories. These categories are narrower in scope and are used within IBM to identify significant populations deemed necessary for business planning purposes. For instance, finance is a primary job category. Its secondary job categories are accounting, audit, business controls, other finance, planning/pricing, and tax and treasury.[11]

The term "career" is often used instead of job category. Each IBM employee worldwide performs one or more job roles and may have many job role skill sets, all with associated skills and descriptions. A job role skill set is a specialization of one and only one job role. These titles describe what one does: what a person's job is.

The number of IBM's primary and secondary job categories and associated job roles may expand or contract over time as changes in the business dictate a need for more or fewer job roles. Each employee is in a particular job role, depending both on the skills and experiences that employee possesses and the needs of the business. How long a given employee stays in a particular job role or moves to other job roles depends on a variety of factors, and it is this movement that forms a person's career path.

The relationships among the various components of IBM's expertise taxonomy are illustrated in Figure 6.1. In this example, the primary job category is finance.

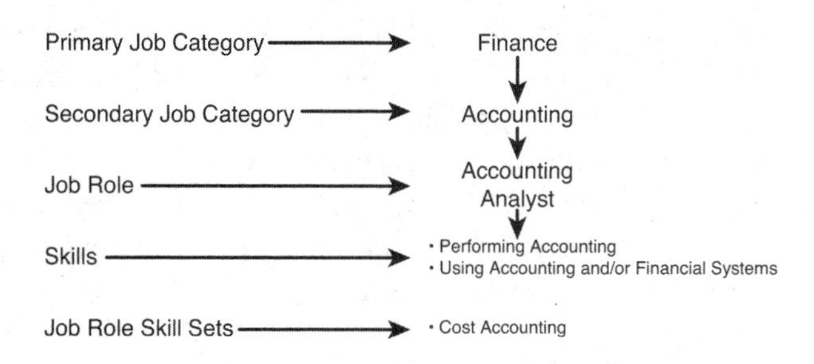

Figure 6.1 Example of IBM's expertise taxonomy.

To illustrate how this works, let's go into more depth with the associated secondary job category of accounting. According to the definition within IBM's expertise taxonomy, "Accounting is responsible for recording, analyzing, and reporting worldwide financial data in accordance with Generally Accepted Accounting Principles (GAAP), in support of IBM's legally required filings."[12] An example of a job role associated with this job category is accounting analyst. The taxonomy continues to explain that

> ***"This job role may include some or all of the following: preparing and recording, on a timely and accurate basis, the company's financial performance using Generally Accepted Accounting Principles, IBM Accounting Principles and Local Statutory/Tax requirements; performing complex operational/technical accounting and analysis and profitability reporting; providing sound management information and interpretation while ensuring high standards of financial control and analyzing and interpreting financial data, requiring knowledge of accounting theory/tax rules and application of corporate policies, practices and procedures."***[13]

Two examples of associated skills include performing accounting and using accounting and/or financial systems, and one example of the various job role skill sets is cost accounting.

Developing a formal structure such as the preceding example of IBM's expertise taxonomy provides a solid foundation for employee careers by providing employees a view of the types of job roles available, the skills required to perform those job roles, possible careers within the company, and the career(s) to which these job roles can lead. Developing a career path based on such components helps employees seek the appropriate job roles and experiences needed over the course of time to achieve personal aspirations and build capabilities that clients value. As employees across the company develop skills and gain new experiences, they build individual capability needed to serve the client. Over time, this collective growth in expertise helps the organization gain strength and increases its ability to meet client demands.

IBM provides guidance for the career paths, which typically contains a variety of elements that are critical in helping an employee progress along a path, build skills, gain new experiences, and advance in their careers. Career paths however, are not prescriptive. They provide career guidance for employees, and in some cases, the paths provide required steps that must be taken in order to achieve a particular career goal. In other cases, the guidance is suggestive, and various options are provided depending on the particular employee need. At times, employees may have to take a detour on their career paths, either because they choose to or because business conditions warrant such changes. Hence, employees need to be flexible in their career progression. They need to realize that not any two people's career paths will look identical and that the best laid plans sometimes need to change. Because career planning is personalized and unique to the individual, the organization's career development process needs to be nimble enough to allow for individual differences and changes in the environment.

Managers at IBM are very involved in helping employees lay out career paths as part of the overall career development process. Managers provide guidance in using various tools to build paths that suit the employees' needs as well as meet IBM's goal of having the appropriate capabilities required to serve its clients.

As already noted, career paths are unique to the individual, and they are customized as part of a career development discussion that managers have with employees. For this to work smoothly, IBM provides guidance to both employees and managers that assist them in developing a personalized plan for a particular career path. The various elements of the guidance that is provided by job category for a typical career path at IBM are explained next. This guidance might be obtained via a portal on the internal company intranet and is available to all employees and managers. It should be noted that the outline that follows is typical; depending on the job role, some career paths are more or less complex than others and therefore require more or less guidance. In addition, while this is how IBM handles career paths, this approach to providing career guidance could apply in many different types of organizations.

Following is an example of career guidance[14] that IBM provides to its employees; it is typically provided for a particular job category.

1. **The description of the job category**—This description could include information that describes the various roles within the job

category and their responsibilities, characteristics of the type of person who would succeed in these types of job roles, and any unique traits or areas of specialty that can help individuals distinguish their areas of specific expertise.

2. **The positions within the career path**—Employees can move along an upward career "ladder," whereby they remain within the same job category while moving from one level to the next. An example would be a new employee at an entry-level position who, after some amount of time and experience, gets a promotion and moves to the next level or grade within the job category.
3. **The job roles within each career path**—At IBM, a variety of job roles are contained within a job category. Therefore it's important for employees to understand what job roles are available to them within any particular job category. Often skills are transferable across job roles within a job category, which creates another avenue for employees who do not desire to "move up the ladder" in a traditional sense, but want broader experiences in a variety of areas. To this end, the career guidance includes a listing and description of the various job roles within that particular career path.
4. **The associated expertise**—The guidance should contain a listing and description of the required skills needed to perform the job roles that lead to growing one's expertise.
5. **Learning activities**—Because employees will need to grow their expertise, they need to understand what specific learning activities will help them achieve their career goals. The career guidance includes recommendations of such activities. These activities could include formal classroom or e-learning training or could be more experiential in nature, where learning takes place on the job through mentoring, job shadowing, or other collaborative endeavors.
6. **Specialties**—Many categories within IBM job roles have "specialties," requiring specialized skills in one or more areas of IBM's business. One example would be a salesperson specializing in selling IBM solutions to companies in a particular industry. The salesperson would be required to grow a level of capability in the specific industry they serve as a way to better serve the client.
7. **Certifications**—Some job roles have certification requirements and/or options. The certification is often associated with an external industry group or organization. Any necessary certifications, along with the requirements for achieving them, are included in the career guidance for a given career path.

8. **Collaboration**—Connecting with others in the company is an excellent way to build a career and explore options. IBM offers employees a variety of outlets for building community and connecting with others, both within and outside a job category. Some of these avenues include participation in external activities, such as industry conferences and events, joining professional societies or associations, using social network tools, and finding a mentor. (Mentoring is explored in depth in Chapter 8, "Linking Collaborative Learning Activities to Development Plans").
9. **Communities**—IBM has also established "communities" to help employees collaborate with each other to learn and grow. There are several kinds of communities, from formal "communities of practice" to informal communities of similar interest. Communities of practice are supported by the business and include subject matter experts who are available to the members of the community for guidance, informal mentoring, and formal community learning processes. The communities are bound by the members' commitment to give back to the community as well as benefit from it. The communities also promote an environment for exploring new ideas through a commitment to building trust and social capital.[15]
10. **Success stories**—Success stories are examples from employees throughout IBM that provide interesting and varied approaches to career success. The stories might inspire other employees to think about how they can build their unique career success stories. While each career path is individual, exploring these success stories is often a great place to start, particularly if employees are contemplating a career move.
11. **Miscellaneous job role information**—In addition to the preceding elements, IBM also provides miscellaneous information to help employees select their next career steps. This information is particularly useful as employees become more versatile and move across job roles in different parts of the business to gain additional expertise. It is also useful if employees are interested in changing careers. This information includes
    - **Common career moves across the company**—IBM provides information that shows where employees can leverage particular skills in different job roles. For instance, employees who are consultants sometimes move into project management job roles, given that many of the consulting skills used in managing large engagements are

transferable to project management roles. Knowing this type of information helps employees to better understand the possibilities available to them.

- **Job role populations**—This listing shows the approximate number of employees who are in a particular job role and includes growth across those populations. This information helps employees determine where there is either job role growth or retrenchment.
- **Job categories by business unit**—This is a view of the different types of job categories that are often found in particular business units. The information provides the relative worldwide breakdown, by organization, of IBM employees in each job category. It provides some guidance on where certain positions and job categories might be more prevalent and also helps employees see how they can move across the business within their job roles while gaining new experiences in different parts of the business. For instance, salespeople are found mostly in IBM's "Sales and Distribution" business unit. Here, client relationship professionals work with integrated teams of consultants, product specialists, and delivery fulfillment teams to improve clients' business performance. These teams deliver value by understanding the client's business and needs. They then bring together capabilities from across IBM and an extensive network of business partners to develop and implement solutions for clients.[16] However, sellers can also be found in IBM's "Software Group" business unit. These employees focus on the sale of software for primarily middleware and operating systems.

Putting Career Paths into Action

In a large company such as IBM, it is particularly important that the career development process be flexible enough to both respond quickly to changes in the environment and also to offer employees the best options for advancing their careers. According to the 2008 IBM Annual Report, IBM had 398,455 employees and did business in more than 170 countries,[17] so the variety of job opportunities is vast. It can be very confusing for employees to navigate across multiple business units and even countries in seeking career opportunities. Without some form of guidance, employees are not always sure of what their potential is across the company. The career guidance described in the earlier section of this chapter provides insights into how a company can provide clarity to employees on the options available to them. But how do employees put all this information into action? How do they determine what the next step is if the options are abundant?

This guidance can be used to identify the options available as part of a career path for an employee. For instance, according to the IBM internal website called "Advance your career," Figure 6.2 provides an example of a typical career path for employees in both human resources (HR) and finance.

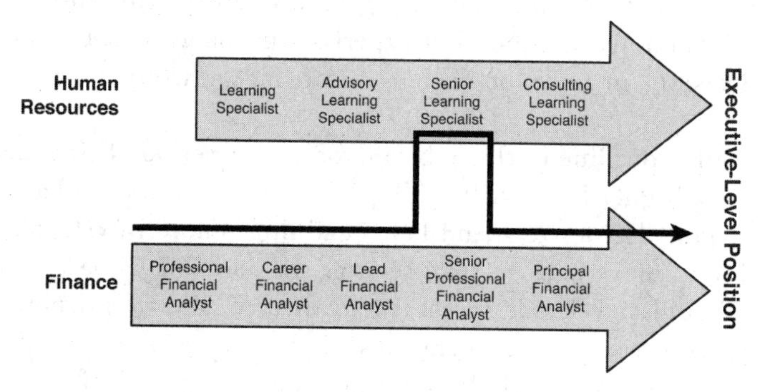

Figure 6.2 Example of career movement within and between job roles.[18]

Employees can spend their careers in a linear path. For instance, let's take an employee, Jane Doe. She's in Finance and starts out in an entry position as a Professional Financial Analyst. Jane can move across multiple job roles and levels of responsibility within finance. However, at some point, Jane may desire a change whereby she becomes more versatile in how she applies her finance skills and decides to move into an HR job role. Another situation may be that HR may have a need for someone with a finance background and seek individuals for HR job roles.

In this example, Jane became very versed at mentoring and coaching new financial analysts. While doing this, Jane acquired good facilitation skills through this on-the-job training. At one point in her career, the Learning team was looking for a facilitator to teach accounting classes as part of the finance curriculum. Jane found that she really like teaching, hence she spoke with her manager about doing an assignment in

Learning as a facilitator. She then worked with her manager on selecting some courses and other possible work experiences to hone her facilitation skills.

After some period of time, a Learning Facilitator job role became available. The Learning team in HR was expanding their curriculum to include a Business Acumen class for technical (non-finance) employees. This would address a need for engineers and other technical employees to better understand the business dynamics of running the organization. HR then posted the Learning Facilitator job role on the internal job posting system. The skills required included not only facilitation skills but subject matter expertise in finance needed to teach basic and an advanced Business Acumen classes. Jane applied for this internal position and was offered the job. Her expertise in finance was a major factor in the decision, in addition to her versatility in acquiring facilitation skills.

Jane could continue in this job role for a long period of time and even advance to a higher level within HR. This could be construed as a career change if Jane decides to spend her remaining tenure in HR. She could also decide to move back to finance after she gained adequate capability in HR. Should she decide to return to finance, she would now have a broader perspective of the operations of the business and would bring these newly acquired skills back to her role in finance. If she were to remain within HR, she could further expand her facilitation skills or even move into a different learning role, such as an instructional designer who actually develops learning activities. These types of moves benefit employees by providing versatility in their careers and increasing the capabilities they personally bring to the table. It also benefits the company by ensuring its employees have the breadth and depth often needed to manage operations in a complex environment.

The example given here provides insight into how a person's career path can have "twists and turns" over time that can even lead to a different career. The employee needs to work closely with her manager to determine whether such a career move is possible and what steps need to be taken to enable such a change. Once it is determined that moving to an HR role is feasible—based on both employee desire and business need—the employee and manager develop a plan that can help the employee achieve her new career goals.

The following sidebar[19] provides an example of career guidance that should be considered as Jane thinks about a potential career change.

EXAMPLE OF GUIDANCE FOR A LEARNING FACILITATOR CAREER PATH

Primary Job Category: *Human Resources*

Secondary Job Category: *Learning*

Level: *Senior Learning Specialist*

Job Role: *Learning Facilitator*

Job role description: An individual in this role applies experience and knowledge of instructional delivery and facilitation principles to increase the knowledge and skills of clients. This is normally achieved by instructional delivery utilizing a variety of methods, media, and technologies. They are responsible for a thorough understanding of the subject matter, attainment of instructional objectives, motivation of students and application of instruction skills in a classroom and/or virtual environment. It requires both subject matter expertise and process expertise (where "process" could be face-to-face presentation skills, e-facilitation skills, use of classroom or online tools and technology, adult learning concepts, and so on).

Required Skills:

- Analyze audience and environment for facilitation
- Apply adult learning principles to facilitation
- Apply coaching techniques in learning environment
- Maintain student motivation
- Perform learning evaluations for facilitation
- Perform learning facilitation
- Perform as learning mentor
- Perform as Subject Matter Expert
- Plan for training events

Figure 6.3 provides an example of what Jane's career path might look like after she made the decision to hone her facilitation skills to compete for a job in HR. She will then need to continue growing her skills in this new role. While this example is based on IBM's career path for a

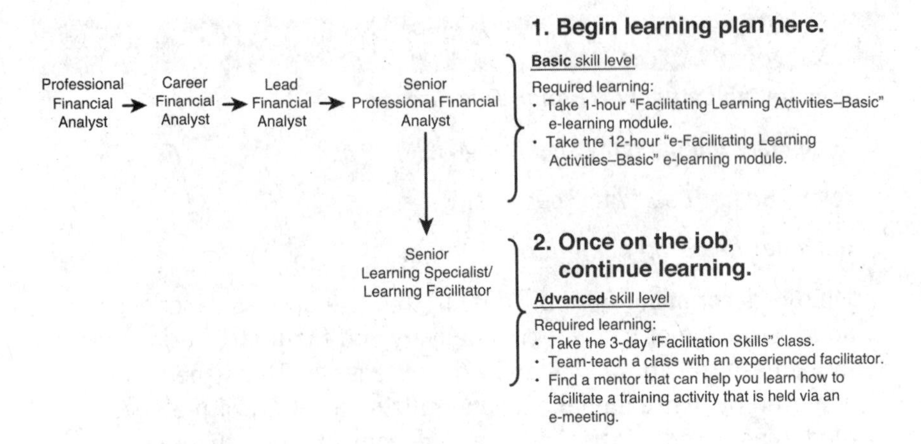

Figure 6.3 Jane's career path, leading to a Learning Facilitator job role.[20]

Learning Facilitator, this information is fairly generic and could be applicable to many organizations. Jane needs to enter the career path here based on her level; hence, she needs a customized career path to increase her skills to be competitive for the Senior Learning Specialist level while she is in the Learning Facilitator job role.

Gaining the Right Experiences to Build Capability for Career Advancement

In Chapter 2, we introduced the concept of a career framework. At the time of this writing, IBM has begun the phased deployment of the framework to employees in several targeted primary job categories, with a goal to expand it to all job categories in the coming year. The career framework is another dimension of the Expertise Management System and identifies the capabilities that employees need in order to provide value to their clients. While skills are needed for an employee's job role today and are acquired through targeted learning activities and repetitive practice, they tend to be learned in a short period of time. Capabilities on the other hand are acquired throughout one's career and could take years of different experiences in various job roles to develop high levels of capability. The career framework provides a long-term focus on career development within IBM and provides the breadth and depth needed to grow capabilities that clients value.

The following section expands upon this discussion and shows how the career framework will further assist employees in understanding what career options are available to them and how they can advance in their careers.

The Components of the Career Framework

IBM's new career framework, when deployed, will allow employees and managers to further define clear, progressive career paths that may follow a single job category (for example, sales) or span multiple job categories (consulting and sales, as an example). This will result in building deep levels of capability and developing more versatile employees. It expands upon the components of the expertise management system that are in place today by enabling employees in any job role to understand what capabilities clients value and how they can grow those capabilities as part of their career advancement. The career framework consists of several major components, including capabilities that employees need and are valued by IBM's clients, an organization structured to support the new framework, and enhanced online web-based IT tools and career resources. As a part of its implementation, it will be incorporated into the career development process that we've highlighted throughout this book.

The career framework is currently composed of client-valued capabilities that were identified as part of a year-long analysis, focused on the client experience. The capabilities include selling, consulting, and providing industry insight, among others. More capabilities may be added to the framework as the work is expanded to include other job categories. There are many benefits to this new framework.

Employees will gain clarity in understanding capabilities (core skills that can be leveraged) needed for current and future roles. They will be able to identify new career possibilities that leverage their current capabilities and receive guidance on developing capabilities needed to succeed. Employees will be more effectively able to define for IBM what they are able to do, and to be possibly chosen for potential deployment to new opportunities. Finally, employees will benefit from more substantive employee/manager career development discussions.

Managers will also benefit from the new framework. They will better understand the capabilities of each member of their teams and gain greater precision in matching employee capabilities and successful client experiences to emerging opportunities. They will also be able to lead more substantive development discussions with employees.

The following processes underlie the career framework, along with associated web-based tooling and a new, dedicated, website that also contains complete details on the initial capabilities and how they are used to drive client success.

There is a new validation process that guides employees on how to progress within the framework over time by successfully demonstrating in a sustained fashion the requirements for a capability at a specific level of expertise. There are five levels of capability, from "Entry" to "Thought Leader." Employees will be placed into the framework based on a set of criteria that includes their job roles, levels or grades, prior experiences, and other related criteria. They will be aligned to one or more of the initial capabilities, with a "major" and one or more "minors." For instance, a sales person would be aligned to the "selling" capability as his "major," similar to a college student who majors in a particular subject area. These are the skills and experiences needed as part of what they do on a day-in, day-out basis. In addition, a sales person might also require some level of capability in understanding the industry in which they sell products or services, hence he would also be aligned to the "providing industry insight" capability but possibly at a lower level of mastery than his "major." Again, this is similar to college students who may minor in a particular subject area and take some courses in such so they have general knowledge, but it is not their major area of study. Together both subject areas provide a well-rounded student, and in the case of the career framework, provides a well-rounded employee.

The validation process is supported by web-based tooling, which allows an employee to apply for a move from one level of capability to the next. Achieving this next level of capability is a major milestone in one's career and could take several years of building skills, changing job roles, and gaining different experiences. Hence the validation process provides an additional aid in developing a career path for an employee, in addition to the guidance described earlier for a specific job role.

The career framework will also showcase a career advisor network, a new peer-to-peer learning initiative, where "volunteer employees" have been trained in IBM's career development process and will answer questions for employees being introduced to the career framework for the first time. They will be able to provide guidance via an electronic chat session on the various components of the career framework and how it can be used to help the individual employee.

A gap analysis is another lever available to employees. It shows how employees can use the framework to assist them with their career development; comparing their personal suite of capability levels with the recommended levels for key job roles across IBM. Based on the outcome of this analysis, employees can build different learning activities and required experiences into their development plans based on a "Career Guide" that has been provided to employees. This additional information provides yet another view of how one can progress in their career along a particular career path, and provides milestones along that path that recognizes their level of expertise and career achievements.

It is important to note that while a career path may have some standard items that are common to many employees, such as learning activities that help grow certain skills, career paths can be very individual based on the skills that the employee brings to the table. An employee will need to work with her manager and/or mentor to develop a customized plan. Chapter 7 provides further insights into how employees and managers engage in developing customized career paths through an individual development planning process. We discuss in detail how IBM approaches career development planning as part of its career development process. Career development planning provides an avenue for employees to work with their managers and mentors on carving out career paths that meet individual needs and allows employees to take responsibility for their own careers by using the plethora of career guidance provided by the company. Chapter 8 then focuses on mentoring relationships and other collaborative ways to learn that can enhance a person's career path.

Managerial Career Paths

One of IBM's primary job categories includes management. Most IBM managers begin their careers in one of the other primary job categories. As employees progress in their careers, they have the option to remain in a "nonmanager" role and in some cases can progress to the executive level in a technical role. In other instances, employees might choose a manager job role whereby the manager supervises other employees or managers (as in the case of an "up-line" or middle manager) and accomplish work through others. Employees that choose a manager career path often move in and out of the manager role and go back to their former careers—or choose new ones. As they gain new experiences, they may move back into management roles. Other employees fulfill their careers as managers. They might also move into manager roles in other parts of the business for variety and to gain new experiences. These various career paths are determined by a combination of employee desire and company need. Manager roles can also lead to executive positions if the individual is qualified for such a role and if a need exists.

Various learning programs exist in IBM for first-line managers, upline or middle managers, and executives, as well as "emerging leaders" or those individuals identified as future leaders or managers in the company. As part of IBM's talent management process to fill and grow the executive ranks, the company is in the process of redesigning its business and technical leadership program that provides a single view of its global leadership pipeline. The program is intended to identify, develop, and retain high-potential, high-performing personnel to ensure IBM has the right leadership in the future. This is accomplished through targeted leadership and business acumen development that helps IBM's future leaders grow and realize their full potential. IBM has created a common and global set of guidelines for the identification and development of its future leadership and at the time of this writing, is currently redesigning the program to reflect the needs of tomorrow's succession planning and leadership pipeline.

These programs help employees move from their technical roles to manager roles, and once in the manager roles, they learn how to be high-performing managers.

Summary

Companies should consider implementing a formal structure that identifies and defines the job roles needed within the company, as well as the associated skills needed to perform those job roles, in order to attract, retain, and develop employees. The extent to which companies do this will be determined based on the size of the organization; however, companies of any size will benefit from some planning in this area.

Senior management must be committed to such an effort and provide ample support and resources. The following is a suggested list of critical success factors to consider in developing an expertise management system:

- Secure senior management commitment, sponsorship, and funding, within both HR and the business unit.
- Identify a program owner, someone with the appropriate authority to manage the system who will be given adequate funding to secure the staff required to drive the work effort.
- Create a partnership with the lines of business across the company. They will be instrumental in identifying the types of jobs needed and developing the job roles and associated skill requirements to support the company strategy, based on their line of business mission.
- Develop the appropriate tools that might be required to house the job role descriptions, skills and definitions of such skills, and employee assessments of these skills.
- Develop a career framework that identifies the required capabilities to serve clients and provides a means for career advancement.
- Link the needed learning activities required to grow.
- Gain the right experiences that lead to career advancement by building individual capabilities that clients value.
- Identify the criteria for certifications, if required.
- Integrate career paths as part of the career development process.
- Provide the appropriate career guidance to managers and employees so they are aware of the job roles within the company, the competencies, skills, and experiences needed to build individual capability, and the options available for career advancement.
- Measure the progress of the initiative for continuous improvement.

Endnotes

[1]Mercer Human Resource Consulting. Point of View. "The Career Joint Venture: Forging a three-way partnership to build careers and drive business performance." 2005. p. 5.

[2]IBM Corporation. "The Enterprise of the Future: Implications for the Workforce," *The IBM Global CEO Study*. Last updated October 8, 2008. p. 14, http://www-935.ibm.com/services/us/index.wss/ibvstudy/gbs/a1030532?cntxt=a1005263.

[3]Ibid, p. 14.

[4]Brennan, Mike and Gebavi, Andrew. "Managing Career Paths: The Role of the CLO," *Chief Learning Officer Magazine*, March 2008: pp. 48–49.

[5]Lesser, Eric; Ringo, Tim; Blumberg, Andrea. *Transforming the Workforce: Seven keys to succeeding in a globally integrated world.* IBM Global Business Services: May 2007.

[6]Howard, Ann, Ph.D., Scott Erker, Ph.D., and Neal Bruce, "Slugging Through the War for Talent. Development Dimensions International, Inc. and Monster," *Selection Forecast 2006–2007 Executive Summary*. pp. 1–3.

[7]*BNET Business Dictionary*. "Business definition for: Career Path," http://dictionary.bnet.com/definition/career+path.html.

[8]Versatilist. Wikipedia.com, http://en.wikipedia.org/wiki/Versatilist.

[9]IBM Intranet. "Advance your career" website, Updated January 26, 2009.

[10]IBM Intranet. Expertise Taxonomy website; "About Expertise Taxonomy."

[11]Ibid.

[12]IBM Intranet, Expertise Taxonomy website; "Expertise Taxonomy Browser, Version M72."

[13]Ibid.

[14]IBM Intranet. Career Guide.

[15]IBM Intranet. Collaboration Central: Communities.

[16]2007 IBM Annual Report. "IBM Worldwide Organizations: Sales and Distribution Organization," p. 21.

[17]IBM 2008 Annual Report. "Management Discussion: Employees and Related Workforce," p. 1, http://www.ibm.com/annualreport/2008/md_7erw.shtml.

[18]IBM Intranet. "Advance your career: Broaden your career web pages," Updated May 3, 2007.

[19]IBM Intranet, Expertise Taxonomy website, op. cit.

[20]IBM Intranet. "Facilitator Zone," Facilitator excellence learning plan.

Chapter 7 Contents

7

Creating Meaningful Development Plans

Having the Right Skills

Today's knowledge and service-based economy demands a radically different response to skills requirements and career development than was required in the industrial economy of past decades. The business landscape requires new and improved skills, different approaches to building capabilities, and fresh, dynamic ways of providing training. Skill development, capability building, and training all come together in a career development or individual development planning process. This is where the organization's business needs and goals and the employee's skills and career aspirations intersect in a plan for how both parties can move forward to meet the challenges of the coming years.

These new and ever-changing approaches to career development and skill building do not fit into the framework of the traditional development plan. Such dynamic approaches need flexible containers that can hold complex inter-relationships and can change quickly as needed. The new approaches are like the proverbial "new wine," and the traditional development plans are the "old wineskins" that are not flexible and dynamic enough to hold the still-changing new wine.

This chapter explores the types of development plans that are needed for today's career development environment. We examine the purposes of development plans and explore the best practices and characteristics of the most effective ones. The system for creating and using development plans is described, with particular emphasis on the interactions between manager and employee that make the planning process valuable for everyone involved, including the business itself. Examples of career development plans and their key elements are also included. And we look at how the new, evolving directions at IBM make the career development planning process dynamic and relevant to the changing business world.

IBM realized early on the importance of learning to remain competitive and has committed substantial resources to creating robust learning opportunities for employees. IBM understands that employee learning tied to business goals gives the company the flexibility to improve or retrain its workforce, so that they can respond quickly to industry changes and emerging trends with a steady pool of highly skilled workers.

In light of the world economy and global business environment, organizations have had to recalibrate their career development planning and the way they view and implement career development. As discussed in Chapter 5, "Assessing Levels of Expertise and Taking Action to Drive Business Success," employees will need to focus on growing existing skills and on learning new competencies, skills, and capabilities. This is critical to ensure that they have the right experiences to grow the capabilities needed by the organization to serve clients. They will need to understand emerging job roles and what skills and competencies are required to fill those roles—and to be sure that they take appropriate action in order to progress in their careers.

Road Map or GPS?

It was not that long ago that people used road maps to plan their automobile travel. They would start with the beginning and end points in mind and then plan the trip in a rather linear fashion. If they knew where they were going, including specific side trips they wanted to make, they could plan that detour in advance. Today, many have dispensed with road maps in favor of Global Positioning Systems (GPS), which have transformed the way people travel. Now travelers can dynamically change plans quickly, responding to traffic jams, road blocks, schedule changes, and so on.

In the business world, companies are struggling to keep up with new strategic developments that often require agile, responsive plans to not only understand new developments but also to translate them into the organization's skill requirements and overall talent management plan. Whereas in the past, the development plan was often a static "roadmap" that was rather rigid and not particularly adaptable, today a more dynamic career development plan is necessary. Such a plan enables companies to continually recalibrate their organizational requirements with those of employees, reassessing the corporate desire to perform with excellence and to understand and align employee career aspirations with the needs of the company. Sometimes, this might involve providing new types of training or retraining for valuable employees, and it also might indicate the need that the skills of some employees might be utilized better elsewhere. Just as the GPS has transformed the way we travel, career development plans must now take into account the dynamic fluency of today's environment.

Understanding the organization's goals and strategies allows managers to help employees map their learning needs to business requirements through the use of career development plans and performance plans.

The Purpose of Career Development Plans and Why They Are Important

A career development plan outlines the short- and long-term goals that align with an employee's current and future jobs. The plan outlines a set of sequenced experiences to assist the employee in achieving those goals. It is recommended that all employees have a career development plan and that special attention be given to the development of high potential employees.

Development plans at their simplest are the synopsis and diagram of each employee's career development for the year ahead. But they are far more than that. When used for maximum impact, development plans are not only statements of employee growth plans, but they are also guides for the manager and the organization, for how they will develop the skills and talent needed to carry out the latest objectives. Ultimately, the purpose of a career development plan is to assist employees in achieving their goals both short- and long-term. In doing so, an organization also increases the likelihood of retaining its employees. The career development plan helps workers set realistic expectations for their career growth by identifying areas that need development before becoming eligible for the next career milestone.[1]

The interplay between the needs of the organization and those of the employee is complex. Ideally, the process of creating the development plan should allow for a dialog between manager and employee to explore how the needs of the department, the business, and the employee are connected and can be mutually beneficial. This dialog is a key component in the success of the overall career development process.

The planning process is an opportunity for managers to recognize all employees and is especially critical for high-potential employees. It is important that managers balance the needs of their teams with the needs of the organization, potentially helping valued team members get useful experience, grow, and get promoted to the place in the organization where they can make the greatest contribution and achieve more of their potential.

Good development plans provide structure and discipline for the employee's focus during the coming year and beyond. Plans that adequately reflect employee aspirations will also motivate and inspire the employee.

Characteristics of Effective Career Development Plans

A career development plan contains the desired outcomes of the career development process and action steps of managers and employees. It is the tangible record of a process and as such is ongoing and dynamic.

There are a number of characteristics and best practices that lead to effective career development plans. According to Robert Stringer,[2] author of *The Power of a Development Plan*, the most effective plans can be described as having seven major characteristics:

- Highly personalized
- Focused on specific development needs and not just summaries of the issues
- Practical
- Rely on on-the-job learning experiences
- "Owned" by the person who wants to develop

- Are living documents
- Strongly emphasize coaching and personal feedback

These characteristics have their parallels in IBM's career development plan best practices. The following sections describe some of the ways that these characteristics are practiced at IBM.

Personalizing Career Development Plans

Career development plans need to capture each employee's unique needs, goals, and learning styles, rather than simply describing the functions of their roles and/or jobs. To be effective, the plan should describe every employee's career aspirations and specific objectives. At IBM, employees are encouraged to answer the following types of questions specifically and uniquely for themselves:

- What are my skills, abilities, and competencies?
- What are my strengths and preferred learning style?
- What are my desired objectives?

Managers and employees are encouraged to consider the following: How will employees know and measure whether they are achieving the goals they have set? What are the learning approaches that will be most effective for each employee? Who are the people they will work with for mentoring and coaching? What are the specific action steps that will most likely lead to the desired results?

Focusing on Specific Development Needs

Effective plans dig beneath the surface description of development needs to pinpoint the specific ways the employee needs to improve. For example, the employee and manager might agree that the employee needs to work on time management. They may jointly set some behavioral benchmarks for how the employee's time management will improve. But what is the nature of the employee's time management shortcomings? Is the employee too detailed and too much of a perfectionist? Is the employee disorganized and constantly spending too much time trying to find things? Does the employee put off starting assignments, spend too much time talking with people instead of getting tasks done, give priority to less important tasks, and wind up lacking the time needed for what is important? These, of course, are only a few of the possibilities, but they provide a flavor for the complexity of the situation and the need for individualized responses.

The specificity of focus can be achieved through in-depth skill and behavioral assessments and peer feedback, in conjunction with a thorough and probing conversation between the manager and employee. As in the example given, if time management is identified as a developmental issue, the manager needs to probe and observe to find the specific problems that need to be addressed in the development plan.

A classic approach to problem identification is to keep asking "Why?" until the root problem is reached. Using the time management example as the general issue, the manager may keep asking, "Why are you missing deadlines?" or "Why are you not getting more projects finished?" in order to uncover the issues that need attention and the best paths for addressing them. A time management class will not be effective, for example, if the real issue is that the employee needs better writing skills and keeps procrastinating writing key reports. But if the need for writing skill training and coaching is identified, then the development plan can include specific action steps to help the employee correct the developmental gap.

Making the Plans Practical

The most effective plans focus on a few mission-critical skill-building activities so that the employee's attention, energy, and resources can be focused on gaining maximum impact in the areas where the most important change and growth take place. IBM has found that it is far more effective to concentrate on two or three key areas rather than half a dozen or more.

Another aspect of making the plans practical is identifying specific action steps and outcomes. It is not enough to identify a developmental plan of "improving presentation skills." The specific action steps may need to be

- Take the Business Presentation Skills class in March.
- Join and attend Toastmasters for at least six months.
- Give at least two presentations each month for which specific feedback is given.
- Work with a presentations skills coach for at least three months to improve skill and confidence in giving presentations, including PowerPoint presentations, to small and large audiences.

Integrating On-the-Job Learning Experiences

On-the-job learning experiences can often be more important than classes and training in employee growth and development. At IBM, identifying and including specific on-the-job experiences is an essential part of employee development. It is critical that employees get certain experiences to build deep levels of capabilities in specific areas where simple training is inadequate. When work experiences with specific learning objectives are included as part of the development plan, the experience is transformed into a learning lab. Employees tend to approach these experiences with greater openness and curiosity, with more focus and intention. The result is that employees identify in advance what they want to learn from the experience, and they seek it out, look for it, and make sure they find it.

"Owning" the Development Plan

To be successful, it is essential that employees take ownership and responsibility for their own development. In many organizations, this process can be encouraged through corporate programs or processes. By providing the infrastructure and support systems to help ensure that employee goals are being met, IBM demonstrates to the employee that the company places a high priority on career planning and provides a process that supports the employee in their growth and career goals. This commitment to the development plan then becomes important to the employees, as well.

Managers play a key role in the career development process by helping the employee put a plan in place and execute upon it; however, in practical ways, employees are expected to set up the development planning and review sessions with their managers. Employees' in-depth input into the plan is expected and supported through preparation and key conversations with managers.

Development Plans as a Living Process

A development plan seeks to identify and record the key goals, objectives, and needs of the business unit and employee. Nothing is static in business or in life, so the best development plans are open to ongoing change as needed. Employees and managers should be continually watching for ways to develop the skills and competencies identified in the plan. By keeping the development plan fluid and dynamic, both managers and employees capture opportunities that wouldn't be unveiled in a static planning process. Once a plan is set, employees and managers should revisit the plan periodically. This reflects the living and changing nature of effective career development plans.

Emphasizing Mentoring, Coaching, and Personal Feedback

People and relationships, along with key jobs, are often the biggest factors in most people's development. Therefore, feedback, mentoring, and coaching are powerful ways to leverage all the other developmental efforts. Mentoring and coaching can help employees see how all their activities and efforts fit together. Coaching could be viewed as a more comprehensive or "meta-activity" because it gives perspective and heightens the effectiveness of all the others. These relationships may also be the only place in the organization where employees can be completely candid about their challenges.

Feedback is the mirror that gives an objective picture of how one is coming across to others. We all have a tremendous capacity to fool ourselves about things we prefer to ignore. Feedback helps keep us grounded in reality and offers numerous ways to keep growing.

Career Development Plans at IBM

What is most important about development plans is that they drive performance and give both the employee and the organization competitive advantage. Employees understand what is required of them to enhance their current skills and capabilities and thereby improve their overall marketability. The organization profits by ensuring that it has the right skills in place to drive client success and overall profitability.

The organization has a process and infrastructure to value the information provided by the career development plan, as well as checks and balances to monitor and track the plan. The career development plan is used to ensure that all employees are focused on their own development and that the high-potential pipeline receives appropriate leadership experiences to expedite their growth and to create an ongoing focus on development. Career development plans can typically be thought of as a benefit to the employee. However, these plans have both institutional and organizational value, and they benefit all stakeholders. As employees grow their skills and are better able to perform their job roles, managers are able to achieve their mission in a more effective and efficient manner. This further benefits the entire organization and results in a more satisfied client or customer.

The following sections offer a description of the Career Development Plan Process at IBM.[3] At the center of the process is a development discussion between managers and each of their employees.

Preparing for the Development Discussion

Before meeting with managers, employees need to prepare for the discussions. The managers might not know what the employees desire, hence preparation will help facilitate the discussions and assure the employees have plans that reflect their goals—and are supported by the managers. Employees will create a plan for current-year and longer-term aspirations. The following steps are typically followed in preparation for employees meeting with managers based on IBM's current career development planning process:

- Review their current year business goals and determine what areas of learning focus are required to help achieve those goals.
- Update their expertise self-assessment of technical skills and competencies required for a specific job role.
- Review their previous career development plans (if they have them) to see what specific actions were completed and what specific actions are required going forward.
- Explore the requirements and opportunities for learning and expertise that are recommended for their job roles.
- Understand the resources available to build and support skill and professional growth.
- Consider who might be good mentors for them if they have not already been assigned.
- Think about what projects or learning activities might help them achieve their goals.

If employees have longer-term aspirations to move into different job roles or get promotions, they will also need to review the checklist just given and consider different options for how they will achieve such. These options are topics of discussion with managers, and some might be included in the career development plan.

As employees go through this preparation process, answering the following questions can help them frame their goals:

- What is taking place in the marketplace that is driving growth and opportunity?
- Which leading-edge capabilities and experiences are required?
- What specific actions enable the highest degree of success in meeting business goals while aligning with personal career aspirations?
- Are there stretch assignments, job rotations, and/or special projects available that would contribute to building capability and expertise?

Holding the Development Discussion

The purpose of the development discussion is to agree upon a set of actions that can build employees' performance, enable them to meet the business goals, and to allow them to advance in their career aspirations. These become the basis for the career development plan.

- **Describing the business challenges**—The suggested outline for the discussion begins with the manager describing the business challenges that IBM will face in the coming year. Because each employee must contribute to IBM's business goals, employees must have the competencies, behaviors, skills, and knowledge needed to innovatively collaborate to bring valued solutions to the marketplace.
- **Exploring the employee's career goals and aspirations**—The manager asks the employee to discuss his near-term goals and long-term career aspirations, as well as to reflect on the type of job roles or responsibilities he aspires to in his career. It is important for the manager to ascertain whether the employee sees himself advancing in his current career path, moving into a new career path, or perhaps assuming a management position. The employee is encouraged to explore his aspirations and priorities, including expectations and the timeframes necessary for achieving established goals.

  This discussion includes looking at how the employee can achieve excellence within the current job, understanding the additional skills and knowledge that are needed to achieve business goals—while ensuring that these commitments are aligned with performance plans and goals.

- **Identifying the employee's current skills and expertise**—The employee and manager then discuss the employee's current capability and skills inventory. They discuss aspects of the current job tasks, roles, and responsibilities, what employees are passionate about, and what they feel they do best. They look at skills and capability areas that need improvement and talk about the outcomes of current skill assessments and/or other organizational skill inventories. Finally, the manager asks questions about how the employee thinks her peers would evaluate her current job, career proficiency, and competencies.
- **Identifying and prioritizing competency and skill gaps**—After discussing current skills and competencies, the employee is then asked to identify competency or skill gaps that she feels needs immediate attention in her current career development plan. She is asked to focus on and prioritize the most critical competencies and skills that are needed to meet business goals and satisfy career and professional goals, as well as the job skills and knowledge that must be developed during the current year's cycle to meet stated performance goals.
- **Identifying possible actions**—Once the gaps are identified, the next step is to identify actions that can close the prioritized development gaps. Through discussions with his manager, mentor, and/or coach, the employee determines those job or professional areas in IBM about which he needs more information and where it can be obtained. They also explore potential stretch assignments and job rotations available within the current department or organization that could help clarify career aspirations or build competencies, skills, and knowledge.
- **Prioritizing and choosing development action steps**—The employee and manager discuss and prioritize the best available actions to close the gaps and that best contribute to the employee's career aspirations and provide optimal results to meet current business goals. The manager assigns ownership for action plans by determining which actions require manager support and/or approval and which actions will be owned and executed by the employee alone.

After the discussion with the manager, the employee sets in motion the career development plan that outlines the specific set of activities that will be accomplished within the next 12 to 18 months. The plan can be documented in an online IT application and stored for future reference as the activities are completed. It is periodically reviewed and refined to ensure that it truly reflects the ongoing developmental needs of the employee. The following examples demonstrate the substantive set of activities included in a career development plan; the first for a Software Engineer and the second for a Human Resource Generalist.

Software Engineer, Richard Wang

Richard Wang (fictitious) is a Software Engineer. In this role, he is a team lead, responsible for delivering on-demand computing solutions. His team has been researching and matching on-demand computing technologies to meet various clients' requirements. His development goal is to enhance both his technical and his collaborative skills in a diverse work environment. His aspirations include leading increasingly challenging projects in order to advance in his career. Richard's goals align well with his manager's goals, delivering innovative on-demand computing solutions for customers working with IBM developers and services professionals. Susan, his manager, surmises that with increasing emphasis on globalization, she will probably be managing a much larger department with members in many countries by next year.

Richard and Susan, as part of the annual development planning cycle, discuss Richard's goals as well as Susan's vision of the department's growth within the next year. Richard has expressed a firm desire to assume a global leadership position in the expanded department by becoming a recognized technical expert.

After their discussion, Richard formally documented his development goals and needs for the year. His plan focuses on the critical activities that must be done to ensure alignment with the business and department strategy of designing on-demand computing technologies and helps him have the necessary tools for meeting his overall career aspirations, as shown in Table 7.1.

Table 7.1 Richard Wang's Career Development Plan, Year 1

Category	Action Steps	Date
DEVELOPMENT GOALS	Achieving the next level during the next promotion review cycle	Next 18 months
	Becoming a global team lead	
	Developing collaborative skills in a diverse work environment	
	Becoming Sun Shine System-certified	

Table 7.1 Richard Wang's Career Development Plan, Year 1

Category	Action Steps	Date
SKILLS & DEVELOPMENT NEEDS	Continuing to build object-oriented SW design skills through macro and micro design phases of a project lifecycle Building on his familiarity with J2EE design best practices Acquiring additional leadership and managerial skills	12-month plan
FOCUS AREAS	Preparing for Sun Shine Systems certification using the book *Head First Servlets & JSP, Passing the Sun Shine Certified Web Component Developer Exam*	February
	Finding a mentor within his organization to help him with his collaborative skills in a diverse global environment	March
	Completing appropriate self-study through Rod Johnson's books on object-oriented design	May
	Reviewing the Competencies Teamwork and Collaboration QuickView and the Building Collaborative Relationships Experiential Learning Activity (ELA)	July
	Exploring the business acumen resources to build business skills	August
	Learning how to leverage and maximize team member expertise to accomplish goals	Ongoing
	Attend a global leadership program at a university	October

Throughout the year, Richard executed his plan and had periodic discussions with his manager and mentor to ensure he stayed on track. After a year, Richard was very successful in his job performance and completed nearly all of his development goals. Susan's foresight was right on target. With her increased responsibilities it became clear that Susan did need a global team lead, so she posted the job, and she and two peer managers interviewed the top five candidates. After completing the global search it became very clear to Susan, her peer managers, and her management chain that Richard was the best qualified candidate for the job. So she promoted Richard to lead the global team.

In Year 2, Richard Wang is now a global team lead as a Software Engineer, with team members in four countries. He's responsible for delivering on-demand computing solutions to a major Fortune 500 client.

Susan's department goals of delivering the highest quality on-demand computing solutions remains the same, but the need for increasing client satisfaction while reducing cost is growing.

In his first year as a global team lead, Richard's primary development goal is to continue to enhance his collaborative skills in a globally diverse work environment. He has also expressed an interest in continuing to lead increasingly challenging projects. He wants to be a more effective negotiator and would like to have more opportunities to lead complex projects. His goals and development needs for this year follow in Table 7.2.

Table 7.2 Richard Wang's Career Development Plan, Year 2

Category	Action Steps	Date
DEVELOPMENT GOALS	Advancing project management skills	Next 24 months
	Enhancing collaborative skills in a diverse work environment	
	Developing the lead-certified specialists in Sun Shine Systems and helping the team to become certified	
SKILLS & DEVELOPMENT NEEDS	Continuing to build his collaborative skills and influence by working with and establishing a partnership with more experienced successful team leaders	12 months
	Training on negotiating and presentation skills to executive management	
	Building on leadership and managerial skills	
	Attending the monthly management development seminar	
FOCUS AREAS	Preparing for management seminars by doing online pre-work and presenting at seminars	Ongoing

Table 7.2 Richard Wang's Career Development Plan, Year 2

Category	Action Steps	Date
	Completing research and being chosen to present at upcoming technical conference	March
	Exploring opportunities with experienced team leaders to build collaborative skills	May–Ongoing
	Continuing to meet with mentor within his organization to help him with his collaborative skills in a diverse global environment	Quarterly meetings
	Mentor others to meet their goals	Ongoing

In Richard's new global team role, he is responsible for leading, integrating, and ensuring collaboration to meet his client goals and achieve business success. This requires him to focus on a different skill set, one in which he not only exhibits the technical know-how, but also one in which he works through others to ensure that they have the necessary collaborative as well as technical ability to meet the business goals. His career development goals for the new year shift to align more with his leadership responsibilities, as well as positioning him to meet his personal longer-term career aspirations.

Human Resource Generalist, Bonnie Lawson

Bonnie Lawson (fictitious) is a Human Resource Generalist. In this role, she is responsible for supporting a major business unit and the executive management team. Her team relies on her to support the compensation strategy and compensation cycle, the implementation of their talent management strategy, and monitoring the performance management processes for their business. Ron, Bonnie's manager, has discussed with Bonnie the importance of responsiveness and delivering excellence to the executive team. Ron stresses that before Bonnie has the opportunity to move to a new area within HR, she must demonstrate excellence in the execution of her current responsibilities. Ron agrees that a focus on building organizational capacity would be a good next-step opportunity for Bonnie. This focus would not only benefit the organization, but is an area that Ron sees as a critical need within the current HR team.

Bonnie and Ron, as part of the annual development planning cycle, discuss Bonnie's goals as well as Ron's vision of the department's growth within the next year. Bonnie understands that it is critical for her to exceed her performance goals and deliver with excellence. After their discussion, Bonnie formally documented her development goals and needs for the year as shown in Table 7.3.

Table 7.3 Bonnie Lawson's Career Development Plan, Year 1

Category	Action Steps	Date
DEVELOPMENT GOALS	Developing understanding of organizational requirements and the implications and impact on the talent strategy	Over next 18 months
	Becoming a subject matter expert leader within the HR community	
SKILLS & DEVELOPMENT NEEDS	Continuing to increase knowledge and understanding of talent management	12 months
	Performing business analysis	
	Appling consulting methodologies	
	Understanding collaborative influence	
FOCUS AREAS	Developing a strategic view of business requirements	March
	Working on cross-functional projects to expand knowledge of business	May–August
	Meeting with mentor to discover and review strategies and approaches	Monthly
	Continuing to meet business and personal goals in a timely and professional manner	Ongoing
	Attending workshop on a consultative approach to leadership	October

Bonnie is very focused on meeting business needs while ensuring that she also stays aligned with her personal career development needs. Bonnie executes her plan and has quarterly discussions with her manager and monthly discussions with her mentor to ensure that she is on track. At the end of the year, during Bonnie's self-assessment, she realizes that she did not meet all of her performance objectives. Even though she focused on her career development needs, she was not able to complete all items to her satisfaction. When Bonnie met with her manager, Ron, she reviewed her business challenges and discussed what she would need to do to get on target. Ron agreed with Bonnie's assessment and further felt that Bonnie would gain from a hands-on opportunity while working on a special project. They both agreed to look for the right project that would give Bonnie the specific expertise that would benefit her. Ron felt that Bonnie had the necessary expertise and competencies to work successfully on a cross-functional team and would do extremely well on the special project as detailed in Table 7.4.

Table 7.4 Bonnie Lawson's Career Development Plan, Year 2

Category	Action Steps	Date
DEVELOPMENT GOALS	Advancing project management skills	Next 12 months
	Enhancing collaborative skills	
	Understanding HR policies and practices	
SKILLS & DEVELOPMENT NEEDS	Understanding the core capabilities of IBM and business unit-specific needs	12 months
	Understanding IBM's organizational structure and key HR roles to gain insights for creating future partnerships and collaboration opportunities	
	Enhancing ability to be make presentations	
FOCUS AREAS	Working with mentor to expand HR network	Ongoing
	Completing business acumen curriculum to build business skills	March–May
	Completing the time management learning activity	
	Learning more about IBM's business through working with subject matter experts on special projects	July
	Completing presentation learning activity and presenting at key meetings	September

Although Bonnie did not meet all of her business and development goals, she learned and grew from the challenges of the business. She rededicated herself to maintaining high performance while doing those activities that enhance her performance and career development needs.

Development planning and career opportunities are very individualized and don't always mean moving from one promotion to the next. As we see in this scenario with Bonnie, growth came in her self-assessment, the discussion, and feedback with her manager and mentor, and her willingness to learn from her experience. Bonnie's willingness to work on a project with more experienced employees will give her insights that will be prove to be very beneficial in her growth and development.

Future Directions for Career Development Plans at IBM

This chapter discussed IBM's historic approach to career development plans and the impact they can have on employees' career advancement. In 2008, Human Resources (HR) began a journey to study the effectiveness of the current process and online IT application used by employees to record their career development plans. Various key indicators—from anecdotal manager and employee input to numerous related studies done over recent years—indicated changes were warranted. Hence, in October 2008, HR conducted a comprehensive survey and invited over 1,000 IBM managers and employees across the different business units and geographical locations to determine how the company could enhance the career development planning process and online IT application.

The results of this survey provided valuable insights into program and process changes that will result in an overhaul of the career development planning process and online IT application. Some of the changes that will be reflected in the new process and associated tools include

- Better enablement of ongoing discussions with manager, coaches, mentors, and colleagues, with more meaningful and realistic feedback and planning
- Increased emphasis on networking with colleagues via communities, authoring/patenting, and other experiential learning activities
- An extension of the business planning process, connecting business objectives and personal growth to ensure a closed-loop process
- Stronger integration with other career development online IT applications and programs, including Expertise Management (skills, capabilities, and competencies)
- A dynamic, ongoing process with checkpoints for the employee and manager to ensure employees stay on track with their development and managers are enabled to support them

- Enhanced management support by revitalizing the management community with best practices
- An expansive view of what career development means that includes formal and informal learning, expertise growth, potential project opportunities and job roles, and participation in talent programs including those for business and technical leadership[4]
- Updated program measurements to reflect the new facets of the program to ensure that it stays fresh and continues to meet the needs of employees and IBM

Summary

At IBM, the plan and the process of creating meaningful development plans provide a variety of benefits for employees, managers, and business leaders.[5]

Employees get help exploring what they want in their careers, learn what their career options are, see how to achieve their goals, and discover ways to manage their own careers. They learn how to clearly communicate their interests and aspirations, to managers, mentors, and colleagues. They become more aware of resources (programs, people, content, tools) available and how to take advantage of them. And they understand the way to align their career development with the IBM business and get feedback on areas for improvement. Managers can better prepare their teams to align with the expertise required in the marketplace and that is valued by clients and are better equipped to guide and coach employees. They know what their employees want in their careers and can leverage their interests with business talent requirements that drive organizational goals.

Business leaders are provided with a process to ensure development planning is aligned with business objectives and client value. They receive better information and can make better workforce management decisions (including expertise management, ensuring retention of key talent, and so on). They are better able to optimize learning and development investments and have more flexibility in how to conduct the employee development process in their businesses.

Most employees are genuinely looking for ways to improve their performance by enhancing their expertise. They do this through many of the suggestions that have been outlined in the previous chapters. The career development plan is a way for employees to reflect upon their needs and aspirations and align them with the goals of the organization. A meaningful development plan creates a platform to discuss with their managers, mentors—and others who are instrumental in supporting employees as they move forward in achieving their career milestones. The plan needs to be reviewed and refreshed on a periodic basis so that it does not become stale or outdated and to help ensure that employees have taken action on their plans.

In Chapter 8, "Linking Collaborative Learning Activities to Development Plans," we continue the discussion of career development planning by looking at the many innovative ways beyond the typical classroom training by which employees can learn new skills. These types of innovative learning offer employees a robust array of opportunities to get closer to reaching their career goals.

Endnotes

[1]Communicating about Performance (Career Development Plans) Manager's Toolkit, IBM, 2008.

[2]Stringer, Robert A. "The Power of a Development Plan," December 1, 2003, www.albusiness.com.

[3]Communicating about Performance, IBM QuickView, IBM, 2008.

[4]IBM IDP Transformation Team, IBM, 2008.

[5]Bopp, Mary Ann. Transforming the Development Process, IBM, 2008.

Chapter 8 Contents

8

Linking Collaborative Learning Activities to Development Plans

Overview

Many organizations are spending time, energy, and dollars to develop expertise needed to meet organizational goals, a strategy that is of utmost importance for sustaining the right level of capability for meeting the changing demands of the marketplace. It is important to remain steadfast in keeping up with changes in the marketplace, accurately reading the signals, then making the necessary provisions to develop the required capabilities needed by the workforce. A major problem for many organizations is that they tend to operate in a short-term mode and neglect appropriate planning for the development of this expertise. Without a firm strategy for developing the capabilities of its employees, the future seems to arrive at an accelerated pace—and often unannounced, consequently leaving the organization unprepared to respond to the demands of its clients. The resulting effect is the strong possibility that market share will be lost. One of the ways to be better prepared to address the tactical and strategic expertise requirements is to include career development planning in the organization's business forecasting model. One of IBM's principal methods of addressing the need to develop expertise is through collaborative learning activities, which offer its global workforce a variety of learning options and tools. Consistent with this thought, this chapter emphasizes the importance of designing a learning strategy to meet on-going skills needs as well as provide insights on how IBM uses the collaborative approach to learning with examples and illustrations of some of their best practices.

IBM remains mindful of the fact that the only thing that is constant in the global marketplace is change, and the company makes every effort to meet the challenges of a constantly changing world economy. The organization has the vision, business prudence, and foresight to see the opportunities that exist within these marketplace challenges, which is one of the compelling reasons the company invests in career development. When IBM amasses the right skills for the present and the future, it helps capitalize on the opportunities that change presents. Companies that do not make provisions for business changes by having the right capabilities could find themselves overwhelmed and consumed by the unstable nature of the global economy and marketplace dynamics. IBM tries to be proactive by developing the right skills that position the company to be adaptable and flexible when "disruptive business changes" occur.

In a 2008 article, "Transforming IBM," the company restated its position on ways to be prepared to deal with business changes by affirming that "In IBM, we are building a highly adaptable business, tightly integrated across both our operations and the global economy that can sense and respond quickly to changes anywhere, anytime.... More than ever, our success depends on our ability to respond at the speed of the market, at the point of client contact. By changing the way we work, we will improve our responsiveness and productivity and generate profitable growth."[1] Proactive and enduring companies define their talent and expertise development plans to withstand the storms of business challenges that are sometimes influenced by external economic downturn. Some companies act in a state of panic and anxiety during these times and run the risk of indiscriminately cutting talent when having the right talent is the very thing that enables survival and recovery. Also, having the necessary expertise helps the organization to remain steady in its efforts to be more creative and innovative in the ways things are done and to not only see the challenges, but to see the opportunities and capitalize on them to meet business goals.

IBM continues to make great investments to harness skills—such as deep technical, functional, global leadership, and strong interpersonal skills and global business acumen—that give the organization a solid business foundation. When the skills needs of the organization are aligned with employees' interests and when these employees are made aware of "what's in it for them and what's in it for the organization," business goals are more likely to be met. This scenario specifically promotes a "joint venture" between the leaders of the organization and the organization's employees. Mercer Human Resource Consulting defines joint venture as "a partnership in which people collaborate for mutual benefit." The Mercer article continues to explain that "While some organizations hand over responsibility for career management to employees, others have chosen to be involved selectively. Still others are committed to actively managing for both the business' and the individual's benefit. It is these organizations that will win the race to attract, engage, and retain their workforce."[2]

Never before has human and intellectual capital been so important to sustaining business success as it is today, which will continue into the future. A "joint venture" is quite similar to a business proposition in that, as a company invests in the development of its workforce, the expectation is that employees will return value to the business. This approach is a value statement that is issued to employees. It also empowers employees to accept the responsibility of being an active partner in this business venture. Inherent in a learning framework such as this is the expectation of high performance and a high degree of contribution that allows the organization to compete to win in the marketplace. IBM uses this unique approach to successfully shape their employee development program.

At IBM, a core element of employee career development is based on the premise of joint venture, where employees are given the tools and resources to execute a plan to act on their career interests and goals, while managers and mentors are expected to provide ample support and coaching. The essence of this career development model is that employees are involved in collaborative learning in an environment that promotes the transfer of tacit knowledge. This learning model is clearly aligned with the IBM values where employees build relationships so that they can deliver collective achievements and value to the business.

IBM's career development model transcends geographic, cultural, and business unit barriers. The company believes that these factors should not be inhibitors to employee learning and development. In the end, this practice not only enhances and encourages employee development, but also builds the requisite expertise to deliver on promises made to its global clients. Under the umbrella of integrating global capabilities in order to distinguish the company, IBM argues that the "Enterprise of the Future searches worldwide for sources of expertise, resources and assets that can help it differentiate. Finding the right capabilities is much more important than finding the cheapest. These centers of excellence are integrated globally so that the best capabilities, knowledge, and assets can be used wherever required."[3]

Finding the right capabilities within an organization is highly dependent on the quality and variety of the learning and development options available to employees. In the past, many organizations relied heavily on formal classroom education to deliver training and development. Today many still use this method as a primary development tool, but it has proven to be quite costly. There is evidence that there is a paradigm shift in the ways some companies deliver learning and development. This shift relies less on traditional classroom training and more on technology-enabled learning, collaborative and tacit learning approaches. This approach gives IBM the opportunity to provide its employees with just-in-time training and learning that take place in a collaborative environment despite distance and geographic boundaries. The learning and development transformations that are taking place in forward-thinking companies offer a blended approach to learning, which includes a mix of classroom education with experiential, on-the-job, just-in-time, and technology-based learning opportunities.

An approach to IBM's career development is the innovative use of traditional learning tools such as mentoring; rotational, stretch, and temporary assignments; as well as job shadowing, all of which help enable employees to develop technical, leadership, and critical business skills. These methods are not only cost effective, but they also create an atmosphere that fosters collaborative learning where knowledge flows freely among team members.

This chapter addresses each of these learning tools in detail and demonstrates how IBM uses innovative ways to impact learning and development.

Collaborative Learning–A Catalyst for Knowledge Transfer

One of the unique characteristics of the twenty-first century workplace is the growing practice of group or team learning, and in large part, IBM's learning and development program is built on the concept of collaborative learning. According to Payton Educational Consulting in their 2004 article, "What is Collaborative Learning?," they defined collaborative learning as "Learning that is based on the idea that learning is a naturally social act in which participants talk among themselves (Gerlach, 1994). It is through the talking that learning occurs."[4] As employees engage in teams with the purpose of learning and knowledge transfer, the generation of ideas tends to flourish, and at the same time, problem-solving skills, critical thinking, and group decision-making skills develop. Collaborative learning cultivates an atmosphere where all members of the team are not only responsible for their own personal development, but also the development of others in the group. This is predicated on the need for all members of the team to perform at a higher level and improve their value proposition to the organization.

In a collaborative learning environment, diversity and inclusiveness are important factors in the development process. This includes diversity of approaches, thoughts, culture, differences in learning styles, and the general make-up of the team. The resulting effect of the focus on diversity is that the learning experience is enriched by giving participants on the team the ability to develop the skills to present and accept diverse points of views and to constructively defend differing ideas with the goal of reaching a productive group consensus.

When leaders within an organization foster a climate that embraces diversity on every level, it breeds a learning environment that is open to new ideas, which is fertile ground for innovation and breakthroughs. Web-based Leaders' Toolkit, Technology Partners reinforced this idea by stating in their article, "Improving Organizational Performance," that "a diverse workforce will bring the company a consistent influx of ideas for new products, services and/or processes. Research has shown that heterogeneous groups outperform homogeneous groups, if the diversity is managed. With a constant source of innovation, a company's competitive advantage will be enhanced."[5]

It has been a longstanding practice for IBM to cultivate a climate of inclusiveness. This is characteristic of learning communities and learning teams that exist within the company. IBM has benefited by having diverse teams work on tasks that range from the simple to the most complex. Diverse teams tend to stimulate critical and creative thinking, which has the potential to introduce novel ways of solving problems and is also a catalyst that forces people to exercise "out-of-the-box" ways of approaching the way they work. The notion of collaborative learning has its roots in the idea that as employees gain knowledge and new expertise, they make a special effort to pass on this knowledge to their peers. The practice of peer-to peer learning has taken on renewed importance to IBM because there is a pronounced need to enable speed and effectiveness in developing skills that are crucial to the business. This is particularly important in the growth markets. Peer-to-peer learning also supports the IBM diversity efforts because this learning process transcends geographic borders, cultural difference, language difference, and other diversity dimensions.

As the war for talent intensifies, diversity in the workplace becomes a weapon to attract, retain, engage, and motivate employees. Employees want to thrive in a workplace that creates continuous learning and an intellectually stimulating environment in which they are empowered to think critically, creatively, and differently. To underscore the importance of diversity and career development within IBM, Ron Glover, Vice President, Diversity and Workforce Programs at IBM, asserted that "Diversity is becoming a key factor in helping define leadership in today's marketplace—effectively reaching customers and markets. Today, continued diversity leadership at IBM will quench our insatiable appetite for talent and enhance our ability to create new revenue streams, retain talent, win and retain customers and maintain our marketplace leadership."[6]

Setting the Stage for Team Synergy–A Critical Factor in Collaborative Learning

IBM has a long-standing practice of investing in creating employee learning options that are linked to the changing needs of the workforce and equally important, the changing needs of the global client set. In return for this level of investment in learning programs, IBM is expecting improvement in performance and a pronounced impact on delivering creative solutions and services to the global marketplace. The perspective is that the company is expecting employees to demonstrate personal responsibility and accountability to prudently use the menu of learning options that are available to them. The cornerstone of this approach is to allow employees to continually refresh and retool their skills portfolio in order to improve and protect their on-going value to the company. To this point, Price Pritchett, in the employee handbook of the *New Work Habits for a Radically Changing World*, argues that "Lifelong learning is the only way to remain competitive in the job market. You should invest in your own growth, development and self-renewal....Your employer may help out with this, but ultimately the problem is yours. Your future 'employability'—your appeal as a job candidate depends on having a relentless drive to update credentials, acquire new skills, and stay abreast of what's happening in your field."[7]

Today, the nature of workforce learning and transfer of knowledge require more than just the traditional model, in which most of the learning takes place in a classroom and in a formal lecture manner. As stated before, the new and complementary approach to learning in the workforce is mainly team-based, peer-to-peer, e-learning, and on-the-job learning. This approach builds meaning and improved levels of excitement in the learning process, in that employees get the opportunity to quickly apply their knowledge and get immediate feedback from their peers.

Learning and doing allows employees to build depth because they are using a practical approach that allows them to develop early confidence in testing creative ways of applying their knowledge. This learning practice also affords employees the chance to do personal evaluation and introspection about their progress and take the necessary actions to address the pace at which they are grasping concepts. In addition, when learning is taking place in a team setting, peers are in a position to observe how quickly development is taking place and can offer suggestions, guidance, and support to one another.

These factors play a very important role in building individual and team accountability, trust, and the discipline among team members to constantly improve. When teams use discipline to drive their learning, the benefits they derive are high performance, personal satisfaction, and making themselves more valuable to the organization. Price Pritchett speaks to the importance of team discipline by asserting that "Discipline also is a key component of trust. It sets the stage for reliability, for dependability as crew members come to know what they can expect from one another. Discipline fosters a precious internal integrity among teammates that pumps up pride and builds the character of the crew."[8] In short, when team members demonstrate responsibility for their individual learning, as well as the collective learning of the team, everyone stands to gain. These are the expectations of any team that is defined as high-performing and forward-thinking.

Historically, IBM has made it a practice to anchor learning and development on a set of values and basic principles that helped to shape its workplace as high performing. This practice has positioned IBM to maintain its competitiveness throughout the years. The following section includes a glimpse of how IBM links learning and development to a core set of values.

IBM Values–An Anchoring Point for Innovative Career Development Options

In 1963, the author of *A Business and its Beliefs—The Ideas that Helped Build IBM*, Thomas J. Watson, stated that "I believe the real difference between success and failure of a corporation can very often be traced to the question of how well the organization brings out the great energies and talents of its people. What does it do to help these people find common cause with each other—and how can it sustain this common cause and a sense of direction through the many changes which take place from one generation to the other?"[9] Watson's statement amplifies the long-held value that IBM places on developing its workforce by providing them with a support system through programs such as mentoring, providing a robust plethora of options for career development, and tacit learning opportunities. Once employees take advantage of these resources, they are empowered to unleash "their great talents and energies" to make a marked difference in building IBM's competitive strength in the global marketplace.

As noted earlier, a constant in the global marketplace is change, and even in the early days of IBM there was a certain level of sensitivity to assure the continuation of things that made the company endure, while at the same time remaining poised to deal with the challenges and opportunities that change presents. IBM has a strategy to refresh, restate, and recommit to its core values and makes every effort to communicate the expectations and implications of these values to each new generation that enters the global workforce.

In 1996 IBM made a statement about "What it means to be an IBMer," and a key component of that statement is a description of "Team IBM"—"IBMers are diverse. We share and leverage knowledge. We pay never-ending attention to improving our skills. We are accountable. We conspicuously share results."[10] In today's environment, heightened importance is given to the talent that people bring to the teams with which they are affiliated. Teams tend to flourish when there is a common expectation that all members strive to develop and refine their skills with the goal of delivering value to the team and ultimately to the organization. "Teams perform best when the teammates bring a variety of abilities, experiences, personalities, and problem solving approaches."[11] IBM aligns skills and career development with cross-organizational learning, with the explicit purpose of enabling employees to develop broad and diverse skills and perspectives. A primary method of exposing employees to cross-organizational learning is done through on-the-job, experiential learning opportunities, including shadow experience, rotational and stretch assignments, mentoring, cross-unit projects, and more. Each of the components of the IBM Experiential Learning Portfolio is discussed in further detail later.

The new norm for employee development is that it is values-based and, to a great extent, team-based. IBM makes it clear that its employees are valued and that the company has an obligation to make learning a meaningful experience. At the same time, the learning environment is such that the transfer of knowledge among employees is fluid. Consequently, knowledge has a multiplier effect, in that as knowledge is acquired, it is multiplied by passing it on to others—this is another characteristic of high-performing individuals. Again, IBM invests greatly in providing the resources and support to its employees' career development, and in turn, the company expects employees to feel a sense of empowerment and engagement. Employees are empowered to use their knowledge and expertise in innovative ways that benefit the company and its clients. In essence, when employees accept the shared responsibility for their career growth, they become active partners in their on-going development and skill enhancement.

To underscore the importance of the role that values play on talent development, client satisfaction, and the generation of revenue, it becomes necessary to articulate the tenets of the IBM values, along with their meaning and purpose. Table 8.1 lists the three IBM values with a brief description.

Table 8.1 IBM Values[12]

IBM Values	A Brief Description of the IBM Values
Dedication to every client's success	A strong focus on building long-lasting relationships with clients and demonstrating a strong passion for desired outcomes, solutions, and services to make it possible for our clients to succeed
Innovation that matters—for our company and the world	Exhibit a deep commitment to delivering stellar and innovative solutions and services to all clients. To do this, IBMers must be forward, critical, and innovative thinkers
Trust and personal responsibility in all relationships	Demonstrate follow-through on promises and commitments and preserve trust in all relationships

In order for IBM employees to live out the true meaning of these values, they must have the requisite skills portfolio to create worth and meaning for themselves and for IBM's clients.

Career Development at IBM

To get a balanced view of career development at IBM, we would like to share the following input, which was received from two employees highlighting their learning experience and advancement and the factors that drive attraction and retention.

In assessing the perspectives of both employees, it is obvious that they thrive when they have resources and an environment that cultivates innovative thinking and continuous learning. Not only is the commitment of an organization's talent development strategy a tool that attracts, motivates, and retains employees, but it is also aligned with the company's value system to deliver on the organization's promise to the marketplace.

Employee Perspective #1

Kerrie Holley is an IBM Fellow and Chief Technical Officer, Service Oriented Center of Excellence. To put Kerrie's career development and accomplishments in context, it is important to explain that an IBM Fellow is one of the highest technical honors that the company bestows on technical employees who have established sustained achievements and technology leadership in IBM's business. "IBM Fellows are recognized leaders in the worldwide technical community, and serve as role models and mentors to the IBM technical community. Being named IBM Fellow provides a unique opportunity to work on special projects or research focused on developing technical advancements or defining a new direction in their particular fields of expertise."[13] Here is Kerrie's perspective on his career growth at IBM:

How long have been with IBM? I have been with IBM for a total of 22 years, although I left the company twice and have been back continuously since 1995.

How have you prepared yourself to develop your career over the years? I have always been focused on excelling in my chosen work, which in my case is an IT Architect. I have sought challenging projects and have always sought to grow my skills. In addition, I often seek to do things (take risks) that I have not done before to grow my skills and capabilities. Secondly, I observe and learn from others whose skills and performance I admire. More importantly, I have always owned my own career, and I have never delegated this to others, not my manager, nor my various mentors. I have always recognized that it is my career and my responsibility. Consequently, I have measured myself on what I can do; that is, I look each year and ask myself how much stronger or better am I than the previous year? What can I do now that I could not do two years ago, and I assess myself in the context of where is the marketplace going and what is of value. I understand this better by observing top senior talent in my own company and other companies in what skills they exercise and leverage.

How do you keep your portfolio competitive with "hot" skills? It has always been clear to me that, as with any profession, I must constantly engage with clients, read trade journals, magazine articles, books to both understand the industry, my profession, and what others were thinking. Early in my career I read a technical book a month and sometimes at least 20 books a year. Often for many of these books, I re-read them multiple times to learn a topic or subject matter. I made it a point that when I entered a class I would have working knowledge of the subject matter, and the class was a vehicle for me to learn even more from the instructor and use the labs to cement my skills. I am in a constant state of learning, all the while keeping and growing a core set of skills. I also recognize the need for soft and hard skills, so I am always looking to add new skills in both categories to my repertoire. I keep competitive by applying my skills constantly and by taking on an ever-increasing set of challenges. I also find time to teach and write because I know these channels are a great way to think and exercise skills in addition to applied work.

How often do you make a personal assessment of your skills to ensure you remain competitive and valuable to the business? I look at my skills constantly and make a self-assessment annually, although earlier in my career it was every six months.

How does IBM provide you with tools, resources, and support to achieve your career goals and if so, how? IBM has a plethora of information that is the best in the world at keeping current and growing skills. IBM provides materials in every imaginable form, from white papers to books, audio, video, virtual class room, wikis, forums, etc. In addition, IBM does technology outlooks and always has people looking ahead. So there is more than enough information in IBM that can make a difference. When you couple that with the large pool of mentors and the professional development materials available, you clearly have a corporate culture devised to grow people and offer the savvy professional more than enough tools. Hence the key for IBMers is to sort through the vast amount of data. The other learning is that people must own their development and stop treating their Individual Development Plan as a corporate requirement or as an education plan, but really treat it as a development plan with measurable goals that requires constant refinement.

An IBM Fellow is a highly esteemed appointment. What career planning did you do over the years to prepare you to get to this level? It starts with a commitment to excellence to strive and seek to be the very best at what you do. It helps to like what you do, and it's important to take lots of risks, prudent risks, which build reputations, build skills, and add value. Having a commitment and passion for IBM's success spurs leadership and is a key IBM Fellow attribute.

Could you give me a quote on your personal perspective of career development in IBM? IBM's size and vastness in people, resources, and technology can be viewed as an opportunity or inhibitor to career development, but for the prudent professional there is no better place in the world to rapidly grow your technical capabilities, skills, and career.

Employee Perspective #2

Jennifer Pelham is a recent IBM hire, and her current position is Career Framework Program Manager, Human Resources. Jennifer provided a quote that elaborates on the point that career development is an essential factor in the recruitment process:

"One of the major attractions of a career at IBM is the opportunity for growth. I left my previous employer partly because I felt there was little room to expand my horizons. I wanted to work for a company that valued my development as a professional. I distinctly remember getting the impression at the interview with my soon-to-be manager that IBM was a place where I could explore my interests in management and leadership. And in my short time at IBM, I have been able to see the reality of career development in action."

Exploring Ways IBM Uses Innovative Approaches to Facilitate Learning and Development

Table 8.2 describes the key components of IBM's Learning Portfolio, and it is defined as learning through practice, observation, and personal discovery. A major element of this type of learning is built on the premise that the learner has the opportunity to reflect and do a personal assessment soon after the experience takes place. In addition, the learner is in a position to receive meaningful and immediate feedback regarding the learning experience. The table lists the experiential learning options that IBMers are able to use to acquire new skills. These options have proven to have notable impact on career development and are structured in such a way that employees find it easy to incorporate these plans in their development goals. These examples also show that employee learning is truly a joint venture within IBM, primarily because employees, managers, and mentors must work together to gain the greatest benefit from on-the-job learning experiences. (Also see the "Other Experiential Learning Options" section later in this chapter.)

Table 8.2 Experiential Learning Options at IBM

Activity	Definition
Mentoring	Mentoring is a developmental relationship between two people in which the experienced person is transferring skills and experiences to the less-experienced person. At IBM this definition has been expanded to include different forms of mentoring such as group mentoring, speed, reverse, and cross-geography mentoring.

Table 8.2 Experiential Learning Options at IBM

Activity	Definition
Job Rotation	Job rotation is a means to help employees develop new expertise and broad exposure to different parts of an organization. In addition, it allows an employee the opportunity to expand their professional network and support system. As employees transition from one assignment to the next, they expand their knowledge while acquiring practical on-the-job experience.
Stretch Assignments	Stretch assignment is the means by which employees are challenged to expand themselves by taking on additional assignments with increased scope and complexity. Employees who accept stretch assignments show flexibility by moving out of their comfort zones to acquire new skills. Managers and mentors should provide support to employees who have taken on these assignments, and the purpose is to ensure that the stretch assignment is a rewarding learning experience.
Job Shadowing	Job shadowing is a work experience in which an employee observes another person in order to grasp new knowledge and get exposure to how tasks are performed.
Cross-Unit Projects	Cross-unit project is an opportunity for employees to work across business units or across organizations on joint projects. The opportunity to works on cross-unit projects gives employees a broader view of the organization and allows them to work with diverse teams.
Patents and Publications	Patents and Publication are a means of helping employees, particularly technical employees, to build their technical portfolios. As employees give birth to innovative ideas, they are encouraged to document and submit these ideas to the IBM Intellectual Property team for evaluation. Also, employees who are experts on technical and business topics are encouraged to publish articles to share their knowledge and enhance their resumes.
Temporary Assignments	Temporary assignments allow employees to take on relatively short-term tasks during which they can gain visibility, expand their networks, and acquire new skills.

Looking at IBM's Experiential Learning Portfolio in More Detail

While explicit learning is a critical component of the IBM career development process, great premium has been placed on tacit and experiential learning. It is the belief that when employees learn together and work together, the learning experience is heightened. The Experiential Learning Portfolio at IBM is also constructed on the premise that when employees learn together, learning and application occur at a more rapid pace than when individuals learn on their own. This section contains a more detailed explanation of the primary component of the IBM Experiential Learning Portfolio—*mentoring*.

Mentoring in IBM is an essential learning and career development tool and, if used properly, it is a great asset in bridging knowledge, leadership, generational, and other diversity gaps. The goal is to engage all employees to recognize mentoring as a business and personal imperative because of its power to transfer knowledge, build skills, and promote meaningful collaboration. In order to make IBM "a place to grow," the company relies greatly on experts to pass on knowledge and expertise to build future leaders. Through mentoring, the company's goal is to build individual capability as well as organizational capability. Mentoring is playing a significant role in helping IBM develop a portfolio of technical, business, and leadership skills, ultimately helping IBM to establish itself as a knowledge-resilient enterprise.

In 2004 IBM embarked on a mission to revitalize the global mentoring program, and a primary objective was to repurpose the program to be in line with changing demographics, globalization, talent management, and the need to create opportunities that drive innovation and collaboration. The revitalized IBM mentoring program uses technology in creative ways to connect employees across the globe. As an illustration, the company has launched cross-geography mentoring programs between mature organizations in countries such as the United States and emerging ones such as China, India, and South Africa. One feature of the cross-geography program includes one-on-one mentoring, in which employees in emerging geographies are paired with business executives and technical leaders in mature countries. In addition to the one-on-one mentoring, employees in the cross-geography program are given the opportunity to virtually attend a series of one-hour modules covering technical, business, and leadership topics. The cross-geography program is becoming quite prevalent throughout IBM, and surveys from participants have indicated that the program is having a great impact on building talent and skills across the business. The learning that is taking place in the cross-geography program is bi-directional because both mentors and mentees have reported that their learning has been enhanced.

A measure of success of the cross geography programs serves to reinforce the point that good mentoring relationships result in a two-way learning opportunity. As an example, executive mentors who participated in the cross-geography mentoring program reported that they were given the opportunity to learn the following from their mentees:

- The culture, history, and traditions of the country that the mentee is from
- The business and economic climate of the mentee's country
- The way business is done in the country, which includes the business challenges and opportunities that exist within the country
- And their cultural sensitivity was enhanced

Overall, mentees gained a lot from the mentoring experiences, and following are some specific areas in which they reported the greatest development:

- Gained global leadership insights
- Gained global business acumen
- Developed cross-geography teaming and partnerships
- Developed new technical skills

Another mentoring best practice is that the company modified its worldwide employee directory with innovative features that enable employees to find mentors across the globe. Conversely, employees are also able to state their availability to be mentors. This is especially important because it serves the purpose of fulfilling the requirement for the professional certification "give back" expectation. "Give back" is a term used in IBM to encourage technical leaders and other leaders such as certified project managers to help build the bench strength of their profession by passing on their knowledge to people in the pipeline. This has and will continue to replenish critical skills in these areas, which is a benefit to the company, especially in light of the expected number of retiring Baby Boomers. Another best practice is manifested through the investment the company made in developing a global website that gives employees access to a team of mentoring experts, frequently asked questions, mentoring assessment tools, guidance for managers and employees, and the roles and expectations of both mentor and mentees, to list just a few of the features.

To emphasize the importance of mentoring to the IBM business, the Individual Development Plan was modified to include a section on mentoring where employees are able to list multiple mentors and mentees, along with documenting developmental needs and plans to close specific skill gaps. Further actions have also been taken to include mentoring in the performance evaluation process. This process recognizes and rewards employees who have made an obvious impact on helping their colleagues close critical skill gaps.

The revised IBM Mentoring program is constructed on three pillars that support the core elements of the program and in essence, defines for employees why mentoring is important for them and the business. The pillars are Organizational Intelligence, Connecting People, and Business Impact, which are each described briefly here:

- **Organizational Intelligence**—This is achieved through knowledge and expertise transfer. As employees develop new capabilities, they are expected to share this knowledge with others. As IBMers share their knowledge, not only does this help to further cultivate critical IBM and industry knowledge, it helps the company to develop overall business capabilities. When skills are developed with the idea of creating organizational intelligence, the resulting effect is that it makes the company more adaptable and flexible to change.
- **Connecting People**—Mentoring is used as a means to break down organizational barriers with the explicit purpose to connect people with the goal to create a better support system and to provide increased learning opportunities for all employees. As employees are connected to the business through mentoring, they become more engaged and feel a part of the organization, and this is especially true for those employees who work virtually or are new to the company. Also, connecting people through mentoring is a strong diversity statement because employees who represent the different generations and other diversity groups are able to participate and gain the full benefits of the IBM mentoring program. Given the need to harness critical knowledge that the baby boomer generation possesses, it is of great business importance to create mentoring opportunities between this generation and the generations that are behind. This enhances better diversity awareness and collaboration across diversity lines. In general, connecting people through mentoring promotes collaboration and integration.

- **Business Impact**—Through the transfer of knowledge, IBM gains competitive advantage by having a skilled workforce. Mentoring is a relatively low-cost, high-impact way of creating learning opportunities for the IBM workforce. When employees have the chance to learn and collaborate with teams that are diverse, the company benefits through the influx of ideas and perspectives. The exchange of diverse ideas, approaches, and styles create a fertile ground for innovation and creativity, and this is translated into a benefit for employees as well as the organization. Again, the three mentoring pillars that IBM defined are in support of the different types of mentoring that employees have access to (see the following sidebar).

THREE MENTORING TYPES

Expert Mentoring is designed to encourage employees who are considered experts or masters in their disciplines to transfer these specific skills to build others. Examples of expert disciplines include technology, business, and other specialized skills. Through expert mentoring employees are able to transition from the novice to the mastery stage fairly quickly in these stated areas of expertise. This learning process is continuous because the expectation is that as employees acquire mastery in their disciplines and specialties, their professional responsibility is to develop new experts.

Career Development/Succession Planning is a type of mentoring that is characteristic of the traditional one-on-one mentoring, which tends to be long-term. Career development mentoring offers on-going career guidance, specific leadership, business, organizational, and political skills.

Socialization Mentoring is used as a key process to help new hires to adjust quickly to the IBM culture. The approach is intended to help them develop a support system and to understand the written and unwritten rules of the organization. While this type of mentoring targets new hires, it can also be relevant to current employees who are moving from one organization to the next. This helps them to adjust and quickly get connected to the new organization.

To summarize the importance of mentoring, Ted Hoff, Vice President, IBM Center for Learning and Development, notes that "Mentoring is so important to the business because it results in the enrichment of both mentor and mentee. Mentoring allows both parties to step back and look at a situation with a broad lens to ensure no angles have been missed. This pattern of reflection expands their view of the world, the marketplace, and each other—which in turn, builds up skills that forever benefit the mentee, the mentor, IBM and its clients."[14]

Other Experiential Learning Options

In addition to mentoring, IBM offers its employees a variety of means to gain experiential learning. A principal purpose is to offer employees a menu of learning activities from which they can select. This is very critical in the development planning process because employees and their managers can identify which one or a combination of these experiential learning options will appropriately address the employee's learning needs. These options include job rotation, stretch assignments, job shadowing, cross-unit projects, and patents and publications, each of which are detailed in the following sections.

Job Rotation

Today more than ever, rotational assignments serve as an important resource for talent and leadership development and are a great way to accelerate employee learning and exposure to various segments of the business. A key factor in rotational assignment is the articulation and documentation of the conditions of engagement while the employee is on the assignment. Such conditions might include the length of the assignment, whether or not the employee transfers to the manager who is offering the assignment, and how to measure the performance of the employee while he/she is on the assignment. Employees, managers, and mentors should have clarity on the expectations and the role each person will play in this development process. All parties involved should clearly understand the goals, objectives, and specific skills to be acquired on each assignment. As employees gain new skills on the rotational assignment, ample opportunity must be available for application of these skills once the assignment is complete.

Successful job rotation begins with identifying the developmental needs of the employee and then having a discussion with managers and mentors regarding the best ways that skill gaps will be closed through the respective assignments. An important point to be discussed is performance expectation and overall evaluation of the employee's contribution to the business while on assignment. The organization, as well as the employee, derives great benefits from job rotations. Listed here are examples of the benefits employees derive from participating in rotational assignments:

- Develop new leadership, functional, and business skills
- Gain exposure to new business challenges and opportunities to take calculated risks
- Expand professional network
- Get encouragement to move out of the comfort zone in order to learn
- Help expand career growth through tacit and practical learning

Similarly, the organization reaps many benefits from rotational assignments in the following ways:

- Assists in developing the next generation of leaders and new talent for the business
- Strengthens employee engagement, motivation, and retention
- Increases employee value to the business and ultimately to the client

Stretch Assignments

Stretch assignments are another important method for helping employees develop new skills and gain confidence to take on additional tasks that extend beyond their current job responsibilities. The terms of the stretch assignments must be clearly understood by all parties involved in the process, which includes the nature and length of the stretch assignment, the tasks to be performed, who will give day-to-day guidance while the employee is on the assignment, and lastly how the performance of the assignment gets factored into the overall evaluation. When employees are given the chance to participate in stretch assignments, the organization must exercise all measures to set the stage for success. Employees who are being considered for a stretch assignment must demonstrate readiness to take on tasks that are outside the scope of their current jobs. Before entertaining the idea of a stretch assignment, the employee must exhibit leadership, mastery, flexibility, and the ability to manage multiple tasks successfully.

Managers and mentors play a crucial role for employees who are on stretch assignments by being available to provide guidance and discuss any apprehensions or fears concerning the assignments. Like job rotation, stretch assignments allow employees to explore different opportunities for growth and skill gap closure. Employee assessment and feedback should be built into the process to determine if the employee is on track to successfully completing the stretch assignment without having a negative impact on the performance of their current and primary job responsibilities. Stretch assignments are a valuable talent development tool and if managed properly, both the employee and the organization stand to gain immense benefits. Highlights of the benefits for the employee and the organization include the following:

- Employees are able to enhance their skills and improve their value proposition to the organization.
- Successful stretch assignments generally boost the confidence level and morale of the employee.
- The employee's sense of value and overall worth to the organization typically increases.
- Allowing participation in stretch assignments is a signal to employees that the leaders have confidence and trust in their ability.
- Employees who take on stretch assignments have the opportunity to explore future career options and potentially new roles in other parts of the business.

Organization benefits:

- Stretch assignments are a relatively low-cost investment in the development of employees within the organization.
- Oftentimes stretch assignments create a stronger bond between the employee and the organization, which has a domino effect of strengthening employee commitment and retention.
- Stretch assignments help to develop the capability of the employee and in turn, the capability of the organization is strengthened.
- Stretch assignments allow the leaders to see the range of talent that exists within the organization.

Job Shadowing

Employees who participate in job shadowing opportunities typically get first-hand knowledge of how a particular job is done. In addition, this experience allows the employee to ask questions regarding the role, expectation, challenges, rewards, and skills required to do the job. A primary purpose of the job shadowing experience is to gather information that helps the employee make sound and informed career decisions. If employees aspire to take on new jobs or change career paths, shadowing experience helps them validate or confirm whether or not a particular job truly meets their future needs and aspirations. If employees choose to pursue particular job roles, then based on the information gathered during the shadowing experience, they are able to assess their developmental needs and update their development plans accordingly.

When employees participate in a job shadowing experience, it is important for them to debrief with their managers and mentors so that they are given the appropriate guidance on ways to achieve their goals. It also gives the managers and mentors the chance to discuss other career choices if the employee decides not to pursue that particular career option based on the information that was gained during the shadow experience.

Employee benefits:

- Helps employees validate career interests by providing them with the opportunity to see the requirements of the job and how it is executed.
- Creates employee awareness of the various career choices that exist within the organization.
- Assists employees in making informed decisions regarding career goals.
- Expands employees' professional network and at the same time helps them gain a broader view of the organization.

Organization benefits:

- Facilitates the transfer of knowledge and enhances cross-organization collaboration.
- Provides the manager and mentor with important information through the post-assignment debriefing process with the employee, which can be used to drive a higher-quality career discussion.

Cross-Unit Projects

Cross-unit projects allow employees to collaborate in meaningful ways that increase the potential to develop innovative projects and solutions for the IBM client set. The cross-pollination of diverse skills and approaches creates an atmosphere for employees to learn new skills while doing the tasks. Cross-unit projects also expose employees to various experts from multiple units across IBM, which fosters an atmosphere of professional collegiality. The synergy that is created through cross-unit projects instills a strong level of accountability among the team members for their individual contribution, which helps to ensure the collective success of the team. Inherent in these projects is the possibility for more experienced members of the project to provide skills development and coaching to less-experienced members, which ultimately supports the notion of "leaders building leaders." Employees derive some critical career benefits through their involvement in cross-unit projects. They are able to develop a broader view of the organization, build new networks and partnerships, get a different view of the business, and develop the skill to integrate across organizational lines.

Employee benefits:

- Allows employees to develop the skills to collaborate across business unit lines.
- Employees are given the opportunity to work on diverse teams, and in doing so they are able to acquire different perspectives and understanding of business processes.
- Employees are able to build new relationships and expand their networks.
- Employees are able to determine if cross-unit projects could lead to career opportunities.

Organization benefits:

- Fosters synergy and collaboration across different business units.
- Allows integration and knowledge sharing.
- Has the potential to create excitement in the learning process, which generally results in establishing employee engagement.
- Allows other areas of the company to see the range of talent that is available.

Patents and Publications

Patents and publications are vehicles through which employees bring innovation and value to IBM. Employees are encouraged to execute their tasks in a creative manner, and when novel ideas surface, they are able to submit an invention disclosure to Intellectual Property & Licensing (IP&L) for evaluation.

In terms of publication, employees who are experts in their fields have the ability to publish articles, white papers, and technical journals in their areas of expertise. The Patent and Publication programs within IBM help employees develop a passion for creativity, which inevitably creates on-the-job fun and excitement.

Employee benefits:

- Employees gain first-hand experience through collaboration and the use of team-based learning process.
- Employees receive significant recognitions/awards for their professional accomplishments and expertise.
- Learning opportunities create an atmosphere for on-going learning through the exposure to leaders and experts across business units.
- This environment is rife with intellectual stimulation, which helps employees to excel and aspire to set and reset new goals.

Organization benefits:

- Through patents, publications, and cross-unit projects, IBM's reputation to create innovation that matters is reinforced internally and externally.
- The process promotes IBM's technical vitality and critical thinking among teams.
- The patents, publications, and projects contribute to IBM's revenue and help maintain the company's long-standing status in the industry as a leader in disclosure inventions.

Summary

All employees across IBM have access to the various components of the Experiential Learning Portfolio, which makes these options critical in career development and skill gap closure. The learning choices are vital to the talent development plan and are considered relatively low-cost options. Employees have easy access to the various experiential learning options through an "opportunities bank." As managers identify these opportunities, they are posted, and employees are able to apply to participate.

In summary, this chapter provided an overview of the multiple experiential developmental tools that exist in IBM. The choices that employees have to develop skills are a demonstration that the company is sensitive to the fact that learning is not a "one size fits all" process. Offering career options addresses the diversity of needs based on the demographics of the workforce. This chapter also reinforced the importance of the team-based, on-the-job learning concept.

To conclude, IBM's learning goals are intricately linked to its global business strategy, and this is amplified by the company's investments in learning and development. The strategy states that "People must be enabled and re-enabled with the right skills and knowledge to meet the changing demands of the marketplace, customers and business itself. Based on the current marketplace and economic climate, the goal of improving the performance of the business, thus generating more revenue, is tied directly to our workforce and to our learning strategy."[15]

Endnotes

[1]Globally Integrated Enterprise—Abstract: Transforming IBM—Bluepedia: IBM Collaborative Internal Encyclopedia 2008, W3 article.

[2]Mercer Human Consulting—Point of View: The Career Joint Venture—2005 Mercer Human Resources.

[3]The Enterprise of the Future: IBM Global CEO Study: p. 42. This study is based on conversations with more than 1,000 CEOs and public sector leaders worldwide, IBM Global Business Services, 2008, Somers, New York.

[4]Payton Educational Consulting (2004) and J. M. Gerlach (1994). "Is this collaboration? Underlying processes and effective techniques, new directions for teaching and learning," No.59.

[5]Technology Workforce Partners Business Case for Diversity. "Improving Organizational Performance—Sustaining Innovation." Articles written by a consortium of HIF Technology Companies on Diversity in the Workplace, 1995-2005. www.diversitycentral.com.

[6]"IBM's EO Policy Letter is IBM's foundation for diversity." A conversation with Ron Glover, 2007.

[7]Pritchett, Price, Ph.D. *The Employee Handbook of New Work Habits for a Radically Changing World: 13 Ground Rules for Job Success in the Information Age.* (Dallas: Pritchett & Associates, Inc., 1993), p. 42.

[8]Pritchett, Price, Ph.D. *The Team Member Handbook for Teamwork.* (Dallas: Pritchett & Associates, Inc., 1994), p. 22.

[9]Thomas J. Watson Jr. McKinsey Foundation. *A Business and Its Beliefs—The Ideas that Helped Build IBM*, sponsored by the Graduate School of Business, Columbia University–McKinsey Foundation Lecture Series: New York, 1963, p. 4.

[10]What it Means to be an IBMer, IBM Archives, 1996.

[11]Pritchett, Price, Ph.D. *The Team Member Handbook for Teamwork.* (Dallas: Pritchett & Associates, Inc., 1994), p. 14.

[12]Our Values at Work: On Being an IBMer: About IBM W3, published October 15, 2008.

[13]IBM Collaborative Internal Encyclopedia—Bluepedia, IBM Fellow, March 14, 2008.

[14]IBM Vice President Learning and Development. "Working knowledge: executives speak out on mentoring," November 11, 2008, www.IBM.com.

[15]Expertise management: IBM Learning Strategy, June 2008.

Chapter 9 Contents

9

Measuring Success

The Importance of Measurement

In the past, top-level executives and employees throughout the organization were often "home-grown." We've all heard stories about the fellow who started in the mailroom and worked his way up to CEO. As time went on, staying with the same company one's whole life was no longer seen as the be-all and end-all of career planning. Most companies no longer believe that the majority of their employees will retire with a gold watch after 50 years of faithful service and are looking at ways to measure the impact of factors that drive the retention of high-performance employees.[1]

In the fast-paced world of high technology, raw people talent separates the winners from the losers. Organizational survival depends on securing and retaining this talent. We've established that one effective way of connecting employees to the organization is through a strong career development program.[2]

In all types and sizes of corporations, career development is a complex and multilevel process that can involve significant expenditures of money, time, and human capital. Because resources are finite and must be allocated among many competing priorities, the following question must always be asked about any career development process, program, or tool: "Is it worth the investment?"

Answering this question as it relates to career development requires methods for measuring and analyzing its effectiveness. Without ways to measure the quality and impact of career development, there is no basis for deciding among the myriad career development options that companies have available to them.

The three main reasons for measuring the effectiveness of career development programs are

- To determine whether career development processes, programs, and tools achieve their objectives
- To decide which approaches are most effective and beneficial and how they can be improved
- To measure the business impact of the program and determine the return on investment

In designing career development processes, programs, and tools, along with determination of their worth, another important question to ask is, "What is the desired objective or outcome?" In other words, what does the company want to achieve or accomplish as a result of this program? Closely related to that is the question, "How will we know whether we have achieved the outcome we want; that is, have we been successful?" This question in particular can be answered through measurement.

Companies must determine the criteria and standards for success and how those criteria will be measured. This helps to determine the degree of success in achieving the objective, in order to know whether the desired outcomes are achieved.

When measurement is done effectively and taken seriously, it can be a major driver for positive change in the organization. In today's rapidly changing world, companies are only as good as the quality of their data and information. In the sphere of career development, the company that wants to attract and keep the best talent needs to have not only an accurate reading on what its employees are thinking and what they want, but it must also be able to take action quickly in response to needs and wants.

In the following sections, we provide an overview of a career development measurement process, including challenges and opportunities, as well as critical success factors for applying measurement to training and career development. We also share some examples of how IBM has implemented measurements for several learning programs.

Measuring the Success of Career Development Programs

Measurement and evaluation are often thought of as final steps in a process, but in fact they should be an integral part of the planning and design of any program right from the beginning. It is important to determine the objectives and measurement guidelines, as well as the process for measuring results at various levels, or else it will be impossible to determine whether or not the program is a success.

Initial Questions to Ask

From the start, a good measurement system should quantify the effectiveness of the various career development programs, processes and IT tools that support the process. The measurement planning process includes these questions:

- What are the objectives or desired end results?
- What are the criteria that can be measured to indicate whether the objective was achieved?
- How will the data be gathered, analyzed, and reported on an on-going basis, to determine whether the program or process is working, whether objectives are being attained, and whether the program or process is contributing to business results at a level commensurate with the cost?
- Who are the appropriate people to gather the data and do the actual work?
- Are there resources available to collect, analyze, and report data, and then report back to the program owner to make the appropriate improvements?

It is also important that measurement be part of a continuous process for monitoring results along the way. Measurement can be a kind of "temperature taking" at every step of the process to make sure a program is working as designed. This kind of continuous measurement can detect problems early while adjustments can be made easily.

Issues, Opportunities, and Challenges

Effective assimilation, higher employee morale, enhanced work "climate," and improved teamwork are sometimes considered intangible variables. And yet it is often possible to find tangible factors for measuring these variables.

There have been many studies that demonstrate how assimilation of employees and leaders into the organization impacts the bottom line. For example, according to Downey and March,[3] in 2000, Deloitte Touche Tohmatsu conducted a survey, which found that it takes up to six months to get new employees working reasonably proficiently. It takes 18 months to get them integrated into the culture of an organization, and it takes 24 months before they really know the strategy and the business they have joined. Therefore giving new employees and leaders no training and expecting them to be up and running immediately is unrealistic. In fact, there is only a 50% chance that leaders who take a job at a new company will remain with that company for more than two years. Nearly two years later, these same authors revealed something even more alarming: "More than 70% of newly hired senior executives leave their positions within the first two years."[4]

As if these statistics weren't sobering enough, recently a recruiter who was tracking the careers of 150 senior executives saw that fully 80% had changed employers within two years.[5]

Sun Microsystems measured the financial aspect of career development on its organization. Sun asked, "What does this mean financially?" It is estimated that the cost to the organization of losing one person is at least 1½ times their annual salary. This includes the cost of recruiting a new person, training costs, and lost productivity. The average salary at Sun during the study period in 2000 was $70,000 per year, which means the cost of attrition per person was about $100,000. Today it is much higher.[6]

Many organizations today are looking for a relationship between career development practices/initiatives and their impact on core HR and business goals. Questions are being asked, such as: What impact does increased job satisfaction have on business goals? Can we use our career development programs to tie particular initiatives such as increased customer satisfaction or improved teamwork to specific career development interventions? Other focus areas that are sometimes tied to career development that create measurement opportunities for associated impact include the following:

- Higher employee morale
- Higher employee commitment/engagement
- Enhanced work climate
- Higher performance
- Increased productivity
- Increased customer satisfaction
- Increased skills
- Improved teamwork
- Increased revenue
- Lower delivery cost for education
- Lower product/services cost
- Reduced turnover and attrition

Levels and Impact of Measurement

From a practical perspective, measuring impact and effectiveness of training and other career development programs is typically done at various levels. These levels measure the effects of the learning at increasing levels of impact.[7] Donald Kirkpatrick developed his four-level evaluation model in the late 1950s, and although it has since been adapted and modified by a number of writers, such as Jack Phillips, it remains one of the most well-known and widely used models for career development. The modified five-level Kirkpatrick/Phillips model[8] is as follows:

Level 1: Reaction—How did participants react to the program? Focus is on reaction or satisfaction ratings of those who participated, as well as planned actions, if appropriate.

Level 2: Learning—To what extent did participants improve knowledge and skills and change attitudes as a result of the training? Focus is on whether there was a difference between what was learned AFTER event versus BEFORE.

Level 3: Behavior—To what extent did participants change their behavior back in the workplace as a result of the training? Focus is on whether or not people use the learning and apply it to their jobs.

Level 4: Results—What organizational benefits resulted from the training? Focus is on whether there was an increase in productivity, throughput, employee morale, customer satisfaction, or sales. And if there was a decrease in attrition, customer complaints, returns, product development time, or sales cycle.

Level 5: ROI—What is the return on investment? Focus is on whether the return was worth the cost.

Data collection can be considered one of the most important aspects of the measurement process because without valid and reliable data, one cannot draw any conclusions. Data collection for Levels 1 and 2 (participant satisfaction and increased skill) is typically done as an integral part of training or career development activity. Surveys and learning assessments are the most common methods of gathering this data.

Data collection for Levels 3 and 4 (behavioral application on the job and business impact) is done after the training or career development intervention progresses for a period of time or concludes. The methods used include follow-up surveys, interviews, focus groups, and program sessions; program-related assignments; and performance contracting and monitoring.[9]

Data collection for Level 5 must be isolated from other possible contributions to determine business impact and ROI. The data also needs to be converted to monetary values so that costs and ROI can be calculated and analyzed. Rigorous and sophisticated statistical analysis is required to ensure valid comparisons and conclusions.

Sun Microsystems wanted to find out what would attract people to the organization and keep them there. Career development turned out to be one of the top contributors for attracting and retaining employees, as determined through satisfaction surveys and comments from employees. The company's challenge in the current fast-paced environment was to "provide a middle ground between defined career paths and 'figure it out for yourself' development."[10] Sun, working with the Career Action Center, a Cupertino-based nonprofit organization, created a way to help employees become more career self-reliant while supporting corporate goals and objectives.

Based on employee feedback to Level 1 questionnaires, Sun realized that having a Career Services program was definitely helping workers in their development, but it was less clear how the organization benefited and whether or not the ROI was positive. To this end, Sun launched a study to determine the impact.

By taking the reduced attrition of 1% and applying it to the thousand or so employees who annually took advantage of Career Service offerings, the company saved above $1 million. Career Services also turned out to be a cost-effective means for providing out-placement support to employees leaving the company and contributed about another $100,000 annually to the bottom line (versus using outplacement services). Because the total annual cost of Career Services is about $600k, the ROI was determined to be ($1.1M/600k) x 100, or 183%. The value from Sun's investment in Career Services is clear, and it would be further increased by taking into account effectiveness.[11]

While all five levels of measurement are key and each has its place in the overall measurement process, it is costly to measure all five levels for every single career development program or learning activity within the company. Therefore companies must make a conscious decision as to which levels of measurement are really necessary for each program or learning event—and which levels of measurement may not be worth the investment or for which data is not available. In addition, as a program matures, a company could decide that continuing to do multiple levels of measurement is not warranted once the value of the program has been identified. The focus going forward may solely be on continuous improvement of the program to ensure it meets the needs of the audience.

Two essential elements for success are management support for the measurement process and the setting up of a measurement infrastructure right from the beginning. These are important in order to ensure

- The allocation of necessary funding in budgets
- Approval of staff time for planning, design, and implementation of appropriate feedback and measurement processes
- The levels of measurement that are appropriate for the particular program or process, including what data is or is not feasible to capture and measure
- Advocacy for the measurement process in the face of obstacles and possible resistance

- Review of measurement results and support for process improvement

The way in which data is used is also a critical factor in whether measurement programs succeed or fail. Data must be used as a way to support process improvement, not as a way to punish or find fault. Data must be protected from misuse or political manipulation that would advance or hurt particular programs or people. Privacy and confidentiality concerns must be taken seriously and safeguards put in place.

Communication and implementation are critical success factors for any measurement program. All stakeholders must know and understand the purpose and process, as well as their roles and responsibilities, for gathering, reporting, and using data correctly.

Implementation of the measurement program must be rolled out in stages, with carefully monitored pilot programs and feedback processes for identifying and correcting problems from the beginning. The implementation must also be well-coordinated across the organization so that messages are communicated clearly and concisely. A change management process is essential for implementation of a new measurement program to counteract and manage any resistance that naturally occurs when change is introduced.

Measuring Career Development at IBM

Before we describe specific examples of career development programs and how they are measured at IBM, it would be helpful to review the Guiding Principles that are the cornerstone for determining the specific measurement strategy for the various components of career development.[12] The Guiding Principles are

- **Continuous improvement**—The purpose of measurement is not simply evaluative, but is to provide on-going information that can be used to improve career programs and processes.
- **Collaboration**—The measurement process involves input and buy-in from all the stakeholders to get maximum participation and value.
- **Consistency**—Data is gathered and analyzed in ways that allow for valid comparisons and reliable conclusions.
- **Confidentiality**—Measurements and the resulting data are designed to protect the privacy and confidentiality of participants.

- **Objective**—Measurement processes need to be designed to avoid bias and personal preference.
- **Ease of use**—The measurement process should be easy to use for both those completing surveys and for those using the data to make informed decisions.
- **Flexibility**—The measurement and reporting process should allow for a variety of data sorts and reports to make it usable in a variety of settings.

At a more specific level, IBM uses a modified Kirkpatrick/Phillips model to measure career development. For instance, all classes have at least Level 1 "reaction" measurement; an online survey is sent to the employees immediately after the class concludes to get their input on the class. Many classes also have a "Level 2" or test component at the conclusion of the class, and some also measure "Level 3," or application on the job. These latter measurements are collected as surveys sent to the students several months after class conclusion to determine how the employees applied what they learned. Many e-learning activities also leverage Level 1 measurements. Levels 1, 2, and 3 measurements are also captured at the learning program level, where a multifaceted learning program is put into place that includes a series of learning activities for a specific audience.

Level 4 or 5 (business impact/ROI) measures are typically done at a learning program level (versus class) for selective programs due to the investment required to do these types of measurements. Often data is not available, or it might not be possible to isolate the impact of the learning activity because of a multifaceted intervention that was implemented, learning being one of various interventions required to solve a business problem.

In the next sections, we describe two major career development programs at IBM and how their effectiveness and impact were measured. We chose to describe new employee orientation and sales training programs because they represent initiatives that are easily identifiable for most readers. These examples represent the higher, more comprehensive levels of measurement described in this chapter.

We also describe aspects of measurements for two other career development programs—an experience-based learning and a global mentoring program. We chose these particular examples because they not only illustrate most of the principles and levels of measurement, but they also have received national and international recognition as examples of best practices. Measurement of these programs demonstrated the impact on the business and also illustrates the use of measurement to continually improve IBM's offerings.

New Employee Orientation Measurement Process

In Chapter 4, "Selecting the Best Talent and Developing New Employees," we described IBM's new employee orientation program as a one-year learning program intended to orient and fully integrate new employees to IBM. These employees may have joined IBM through strategic outsourcing deals, acquisitions, or through traditional hiring approaches, such as college or professional hires. In May 2002, IBM revamped its new employee orientation program. As a result, IBM's HR organization, along with Productivity Dynamics, Inc., defined a comprehensive evaluation strategy to assess the effectiveness and business impact of this new strategic program. Because this learning program and orientation process was multifaceted and spanned a large period of time (new employee's first year), it was determined early in the design process that a robust measurement process must be implemented. IBM was able to use various levels of measurement to capture not only student reaction and application on the job, but the business impact of the new employee orientation program. Determining the impact to the business in addition to measuring how employees felt about the program and applied what was learned was key, given the sizable investment the company was now making in designing, developing, and implementing the new employee orientation program.

Program Overview

The newly revised employee orientation program was intended to help new employees have a positive impact on IBM's business effectiveness. It was tailored both to different types of hires and to various business units and geographies. It continues to be a multifaceted program that consists of e-learning modules, face-to-face classes, coaching by peers, and work-related development activities.

The primary goals of the orientation program include the following:

- To help new employees learn about IBM's history, culture, and business strategy, so as to identify better with IBM

- To learn to use productivity tools and best practices and to become productive as quickly as possible
- To manage change resulting from joining IBM
- To build productive relationships with their managers and colleagues, and so on

Given the program's complexity, a two-phase evaluation strategy was designed and implemented during its inception in May, 2002. It was particularly important to measure the program's effectiveness very early in the tenure of the newly implemented new employee orientation program to ensure it was meeting defined objectives. Such feedback would then be used to continue enhancements to the program as it matured.

The measurement strategy put in place was comprised of two phases that summarized data collection activities during the early implementation in 2003. The following sections describe these various phases.

Phase One: Time-Series Evaluation Design

In the first phase, a "time-series" evaluation design was implemented. This phase consisted of three major steps—data collection, data analysis, and reporting. These three steps were implemented iteratively, as various learning components were utilized by a sample of the first group of participants in the program. The objective of this phase was to evaluate the first iteration of the program's components by "shadowing" participants through various program activities and making recommendations for improvement. Evaluation data was collected as participants progressed through each phase of the orientation program. This approach allowed the evaluation to be flexible and responsive to the evolving nature of the learning program. It also allowed the evaluation to control for intervening variables, such as business group-specific orientation activities, nonlearning influencers, and so on. The findings and recommendations for continuous improvement were communicated to the program stakeholders and sponsors.

Phase Two: Steady-State Evaluation Stage

The second stage included a more structured data collection and analysis strategy. This strategy measured iterative implementations of program components after the first implementation of each learning component. The tools and evaluation procedures used during the time-series stage were adapted and implemented in this stage. Given the high number of participants and their wide distribution during the steady state, samples of participants were selected to collect evaluation data.

The actual measurements used during these phases are described next.

Post-Classroom Survey

Initially, a 1- or 2-day class was held, depending on audience type, at either the 30- or 60-day point post-hire date. It was felt that the class could better serve the employees if they had some orientation on the job before they gathered with other new hires in a classroom setting. A survey was used to assess participants' reaction to the class and their perception of its learning value and the learning value of other components of the program. The survey was given to all participants upon completion of the class. The questions in the survey covered the following areas:

- Overall reaction to the class
- Learning outcome of the class
- Intention to take action based on what was learned in the class
- Effectiveness of e-learning modules
- General reaction to all components of the program.

The results of the post-class survey were analyzed and reported on a monthly basis.

Interviews with Participants, Buddies, and Managers

As part of the process of gathering measurement data, interviews were conducted with participants, buddies, and managers. A random sampling from three categories of interviewees was selected.

Sample 1: Participants

A stratified random sample of participants was selected from the first group of new hires (college and professional hires). Variables used for stratification of samples were

- **Business Group**—Participants represented 27 divisions.
- **Starting date at IBM**—Participants who joined IBM between May 19 and June 30, 2003.

Multiple interviews were conducted with this sample during the first year of their participation in the program. A subset of program sample participants were contacted through email and were invited to participate in an interview.

Sample 2: Managers

From the managers of the participants in Sample 1, a group was selected and invited to participate in a 15-minute telephone interview. Managers in this sample were interviewed several times during the first year of the program continuum.

Sample 3: Buddies

"Buddies" were assigned to ensure that the new employees connected to others within the business and were available to answer questions. A subset of participants in the sample had assigned buddies. These individuals were invited to participate in a 15-minute interview.

Interview Protocols

Three interview protocols were developed to collect consistent data from all participants. The following list shows some of the topics that program participants were asked to discuss:

- Timeliness and effectiveness of communications about the program and its components
- Relevance of the program to their work
- Overall perception of the program
- Accessibility, relevance, and learning value of e-learning modules
- Contribution and effectiveness of their buddies
- Support of managers
- Timing and relevance of the class
- Recommendations for continuous improvement of the program and its components

Managers and buddies were asked to describe how program details were communicated to them and how effective that communication was. They were also asked to make observations about how the program was working (especially in comparison to previous new hire programs) and its impact on individual participants. Next they were requested to clarify their personal knowledge of the program and their awareness of their role within it, and finally they were asked to make suggestions for the program's continuous improvement.

Participants' feedback and comments concerning the program were summarized and organized as shown in Table 9.1.[13]

Table 9.1 Summary of Participant Feedback

Measurement	Description
Overall satisfaction	A total of over 300 interviews were conducted with participants in the program. A majority of the participants indicated that the program was relevant and useful to their jobs. Overall, participants indicated that they were satisfied with the new employee orientation program and were excited that IBM had put together such a program.
Communications about the program and its positioning	Here participants answered how and when the program was communicated to them and how effective that communication was. It turned out that most new hires received the announcement e-mail about the program during the first two weeks of their employment at IBM. The majority were familiar with the program but did not discuss it with either their managers or HR representatives. Majority of participants did not understand how to proceed through the learning continuum. As a result of continued feedback on early employee and manager communications, substantial changes were made on the timing and content of such communication.
Classroom component	Participants found this component a valuable way to both learn about IBM culture and meet other new hires. Some participants thought the timing of the class was just right and were glad to have had "time on the job" before the class began. Their work experience helped them to put the class in a better perspective. Others, however, thought that an earlier offering, before their workload got too heavy, would have been better. Some participants had their class attendance date pushed out multiple times due to project deadlines and travel freezes. It should be noted that as a result of continued feedback on this item, eventually two years after implementation, IBM moved the class to be held within the first few days of the employee's entry to the company. This has proven to be more effective at getting new employees quickly acclimated to their new work environment.

Table 9.1 Summary of Participant Feedback

Measurement	Description
Actions Plans developed in the class	Participants had mixed reactions to the Action Plans they developed during the class. Some participants found the activity helpful and indicated that they would continue working on it back on the job. Others thought the Action Plan was just a class activity. Many participants did not understand how the Action Plan differed from their performance objectives or their career development plans. As a result of measuring this aspect of the program, communication about the purpose of the Action Plan and its usefulness were implemented.
E-learning component	E-learning was mostly well-received. Many participants said that they would like to personalize the sequence of the e-learning modules. For example, some would have liked to have taken the modules with the most pertinent information first, given the fact that as "new hire" employees, they were inundated with information. "Re-hires," who were already familiar with IBM culture, were interested only in employee-related modules such as performance measurement, development planning, and benefits. The feedback also included suggestions for making the e-learning even more useful, hence over time, the e-learning content was updated to include employee feedback in addition to the recommended sequence for taking the e-learning.
Personal journal component	This component helped new employees keep track of their progress, as well as reflect upon and review the early experiences of their IBM tenure. The majority of participants did not see any added value to using the personal journal. Some forgot it was there because it was inconvenient to use. As a result of continued feedback on this item and the ineffectiveness of such, the personal journal was eventually eliminated from the program.
Buddy component	Participants responded overwhelmingly enthusiastically to the buddy component of the program. Participants found that having a buddy made them feel more at ease. Having this pre-established coworker relationship helped them feel a part of IBM. The buddy relationship was most effective when the coach worked in the same department. To this day, the buddy program continues to be in place and remains a key success factor in helping new employees become quickly acclimated.

Feedback collected continuously enhanced the program offering, and the results were extremely positive. Managers as well as employees felt their input was directing the "new and improved" program offering.

After several years of program implementation, an impact study was conducted, measuring long-term impact on the program. The study included analysis from new employees who participated in the program versus those who did not. The impact data from the 2-year study showed that the attrition rate was nearly twice as high for those who did not attend the program as for those who did and that attendees were over 30% more likely to receive the highest possible ranking on their performance assessment. In addition, attendees had a more positive view of IBM than non-attendees. Comparisons of attendees versus non-attendees are listed in Table 9.2.

Table 9.2 Participant and Business Impact Comparisons

Measurement	Increase in Percentage for Attendees vs. Non-Attendees
Willingness to stay with IBM	15%
Percentage ranking IBM as one of the best companies	27%
Ability to clearly explain IBM's values to others	11%
Were assigned projects more quickly	13%
Feel good about being part of IBM	37%
Integrated quickly into IBM	48%
Collaborated more effectively with other IBMers	49%

Many of these measurements still exist in the orientation program today. As a result, IBM continues to monitor the new employee orientation program and updates the program as needed. In fact, as we mentioned in Chapter 4, the IBM new employee orientation program is currently going through various changes to reflect current and future new employee needs.

Sales Training Measurement Process

Another example of a robust measurement process that IBM has implemented for a job role-specific training program is IBM's foundational sales training program for sellers: The Global Sales School. It has a long legacy within IBM and was one of IBM's earliest training programs. While it has existed in a variety of forms over many years, the changing business and market environment required a new approach to sales training. The prior version was heavily weighted toward classroom time and practice sales calls. It no longer fit with how selling actually happened within IBM, and it was not consistently deployed around the world.

IBM has shifted from primarily a hardware and software business to one that is now over 50% services-oriented. This shift necessitated improving sales skills to create and deliver client value, to communicate industry expertise, to lead clients in innovative approaches to business opportunities, and to manage outsourcing opportunities more effectively. Reinforcing brand equity in the marketplace is based, in large part, on the ability of the sellers to leverage the full breadth and depth of IBM's resources to create value for its clients. As a result, the Global Sales School underwent a major redesign beginning in mid-2006.

Program Overview

At the beginning of the redesign, the Sales Learning organization analyzed multiple sales performance studies to identify activities that most impact sales performance. Findings were validated through surveys and focus groups with exemplary sellers from all geographies and primary business functions.

The findings concluded that what matters most to new sales hires were[14]

- **Focusing on the client**—These activities included prospecting and researching clients and client industries, confirming the client's compelling reason to act, designing solutions and preparing proposals, presenting solutions or product demonstrations, confirming client benefits and value proposition, and negotiating and closing deals.
- **Driving the sale**—These activities included identifying leads, exploring and identifying opportunities, creating sales strategies and plans, creating call strategies and plans, making sales calls, developing the client's perception of IBM's unique value, gaining support of the key decision leader, and articulating IBM capabilities.
- **Navigating IBM**—These activities included identifying IBM resources; determining pricing, terms, and conditions; creating, updating, and closing opportunity records; preparing for cadence calls and managing internal communications.

The approach and activities were validated with stakeholders to build a consensus for what the "short" list of the new Global Sales School learning goals should be. A global summit to collaborate on the ambitious redesign was held, representing all regions, business units, and business functions. This summit cleared the path for the new Global Sales School through sharing the differentiating activities within the context of a process that was perceived as fair by all parties.

The six goals of Global Sales School that were subsequently established were

- Accelerate new sellers' quota attainment.
- Enable new sellers to deliver client value and navigate the breadth of the company through an authentic performance-based and work-based design.
- Create a design that works for new sellers with prior sales experience and those with no prior experience.
- Enable a "guidance team" consisting of a new seller's manager, mentors, and facilitator for critical sales resources to help that new seller learn more quickly.
- Deliver a blended design for Global Sales School that required sellers to be "out of territory" for a shorter amount of time.
- Deliver Global Sales School consistently across the world to further the transformation into a globally integrated company.

As the design of the enhanced program got underway, the team chose the following areas for measurement and used readily available sources of information to generate the findings:

- **Seller productivity**—Quota attainment data was reviewed, comparing high performers to those not achieving desired targets, while demographic data was analyzed comparing various sales roles, experience levels, time in territory, and other business considerations.
- **Seller performance**—Performance records were analyzed for sellers across all geographies.
- **Seller perceptions**—Level 1 surveys that were received at the end of various sessions were used along with interviews with sellers, facilitators, mentors, and managers.

- **Facilitator impact**—Facilitator surveys were done at the end of each session and after all coaching and deployment calls. Facilitator team room discussions provided candid feedback on needed changes to modules.
- **Delivery numbers**—Hiring plan and actual number of sellers who participated in the program were compared and analyzed.

A program such as Global Sales School requires the combined efforts of many people around the world, so adding and demonstrating value was critical. In addition, because sales is so visible to the organization, all business units wanted to know exactly what they will gain. It was important to demonstrate to business unit executives that Global Sales School was being deployed effectively around the world and was producing higher quota attainment from its graduates.

Results of New Sales Training

As the deployment of the new design got underway and some time had passed, various measurement studies and analyses revealed the following results from the newly enhanced Global Sales School, based on the six goals for the new program:

1. **Accelerate new sellers' quota attainment.**
   A study of Global Sales School graduates proved that sellers who attend the school achieved higher quota attainment:
   - 26% higher for experienced sellers
   - 70% higher for new sellers

   This significantly impacted the net profitability for both new and experienced sellers. These are spectacular numbers in terms of ROI. Only a few new and experienced sellers are needed to graduate to pay back the design and operating costs of the program.

   In addition to the percentages and financial analysis of the quota data, the odds of a Global Sales School graduate being an above-average performer were also examined to ensure that Global Sales School "works" for the majority of sellers. This is similar to medical studies that report on the odds of a given treatment having a positive effect. The study found that

- Experienced sellers graduating from Global Sales School are almost two times more likely to achieve above-average quota attainment by their sixth quarter of selling—as compared to experienced sellers who did not attend Global Sales School.
- New sellers graduating from Global Sales School are over three times more likely to achieve above-average quota attainment by their third quarter of selling—as compared to new sellers who did not attend Global Sales School.

2. **Enable new sellers to deliver client value and navigate the breadth of the company through an authentic performance-based and work-based design.**

 The increased quota attainment discussed here also speaks to this point. Additionally, qualitative feedback from sellers found that they mention practice sales calls, navigating the organization, tools/resources, and face-to-face labs as the most valuable aspects of the program. Practice sales calls and face-to-face events have always been popular, but sellers also mention the new elements of the work-based design. They valued Global Sales School teaching them how to operate within the organization.

3. **Create a design that works for new sellers with prior sales experience and those with no prior experience.**

 Global Sales School is for sales hires within all business units of the company. This includes

 - New sellers who have never held a sales position
 - Experienced sellers taking a sales position within the company for the first time

 New sellers are enrolled in a 12-week version of Global Sales School, while experienced sellers attend a 6-week version that omits the more basic content.

4. **Enable a "guidance team" consisting of a new seller's manager, mentors, and facilitator for critical sales resources to help that new seller learn more quickly.**

 Besides learning from their own experience, sellers learn from colleagues. Global Sales School leverages a "guidance team" for each seller, which is composed of his or her manager, expert mentors, and facilitator.

 Managers receive regular reports on the progress of their sellers in Global Sales School.

Expert mentors (appointed by each seller's manager) review sellers' understanding of key sales tools and processes. They are critical because access to experienced colleagues is an accelerator of sales performance. Global Sales School requires expert mentors to review the graduation requirements so they and the sellers spend time sharing information despite other demands on their time.

The same facilitator stays with each seller from the start to the end of Global Sales School and manages the assessment for each seller.

The Global Sales School website is personalized and can automatically distinguish if a visitor is a Global Sales School enrollee, a manager, mentor, or facilitator of a stream of enrollees. Different content and features appear for each type of visitor and provide information about learning plan progress and other pertinent data.

Each seller's guidance team provides the direction and assistance that sellers need to perform their various deliverables. The sum of these deliverables provides comprehensive training on the "real world" of selling within the organization—enabling sellers to quickly conquer the learning curve and deliver higher revenue faster.

5. **Deliver a blended design for Global Sales School that required sellers to be "out of territory" for a shorter amount of time.**

   The new Global Sales School brings efficiencies to the business in terms of effort. It reduces the duration of the training from

   - 16 weeks to 12 weeks for new sellers
   - 16 weeks to 6 weeks for experienced sellers

6. **Deliver Global Sales School consistently across the world to further the transformation into a globally integrated company.** Global Sales School trains approximately 4,250 sales hires in over 70 countries annually—half of them new sellers and half experienced sellers. Their improved performance goes straight to the bottom line.

   In an interview with Matt Valencius, an executive instrumental in the design and delivery of Global Sales School, he said, "Global Sales School, of course, has terrific ROI numbers. But, more than that, the process to demonstrate value every step of the way is what makes the effort stand out. We simply needed the measurements of incremental value to get through each stage of the process. And, these various measurements build upon each other until the evidence is just overwhelming that Global Sales School increases the productivity of new sales hires."[15]

Lessons Learned

Many of the best practices Sales Learning demonstrated with the redesign of Global Sales School are reusable inside and outside of IBM:[16]

- **Be clear on what value the new learning program is intended to bring to the business.** Clarity on business alignment makes it easier to form an effective partnership with stakeholders and to remove distractions. The motivation for the redesign of Global Sales School was to accelerate the performance of new sales hires so that they could help the business grow faster. This served as a strong reason for a performance-based and work-based design and helped prevent the design from evolving into a disjointed collection of disparate content important to different stakeholders.
- **Conduct a performance differentiation analysis before beginning the design to learn what differentiates top from typical performers.** This will focus the design on a finite set of high-value activities. "Accelerated performance" was not sufficient information to build a program around. We needed to know what activities were correlated with high performance and differentiated top from typical sellers. This list also helped us keep the design focus on a finite number of activities—again avoiding the problem of every stakeholder promoting their favorite topic. A performance differentiation analysis can be used to create a solid foundation for any planned learning offering.
- **Determine what measurements will be reported back to the business so that expectations can be set and the design can be optimized to produce them.** Obtaining a measurable increase in sales quotas was always the main goal for Global Sales School—solid proof to the business of the value the program delivered. Knowing that this was the goal early on enabled us to design the tracking systems we would

need to determine "who did what" and to have enough time to work with all the different parts of the business responsible for financial data. It also enabled us to set expectations with stakeholders so that they would "give us space" to create the design and measure the results. We were following a planned measurement strategy rather than reacting to ad-hoc demands for information.

- **Make the design performance- and work-based.** Global Sales School has sellers build skills in the very same tasks they will need to perform in their jobs. This saves everyone time. The design of Global Sales School is also careful to assess these authentic work deliverables rather than knowledge of theory or effort. Focusing learning on authentic "ends" rather than "means" drives sellers to concentrate on effective execution—exactly what we want them to do "on the job."
- **Leverage and reuse technology and applications as much as possible.** Any custom technologies created for the program should be designed with an eye on reusing them on future programs. Global Sales School can be run efficiently due to the many technologies we have created over the years to effectively manage blended learning designs. The innovations and enhancements created for Global Sales School will be reused in future learning programs. Strategic reuse is critical for learning to deliver the innovation and value to the business on budgets that support the growth targets of the organization.
- **Design and development teams should work closely together to ensure that the program launch goes smoothly.** Global Sales School had multiple interlocking teams to ensure that the design progressed from analysis through measurement without important work being "dropped" or continuity lost in the transition from one team to another. Clear distinctions between design and deployment must be drawn for work to be done efficiently. Team members must also be willing to play multiple roles to keep the project moving quickly and effectively toward a successful launch.

Other Measurements at IBM

In the past few years, several other career development programs were implemented that have proven to have positive impact on employees. While the programs did not warrant the extent of measurement that the new employee orientation program or Global Sales School did, results have been very favorable and provide an avenue for program improvement.

Experience-based Learning Measurement Process

Listed in this section are examples of how IBM measures the success of its experience-based learning initiatives.

In Chapter 8, "Linking Collaborative Learning Activities to Development Plans," we described a variety of experiential learning activities that are part of a formal program IBM implemented in 2006. This experienced-based learning program was implemented as a solution to provide a systematic approach for employees to

- Acquire new or enhance current skills by participating in global experiential developmental opportunities such as stretch assignments, cross-unit projects, job shadowing activities, and so on.
- Expand their knowledge and professional development in ways other than traditional classroom and e-learning training and without limitations of country borders.
- Use a "learning opportunity bank" to apply for the various experiential developmental opportunities available on a global basis.

The program connected employees to global business opportunities, enabling them to find the best alternatives for personal career growth, skill and expertise development, and created an optimal experiential solution based on individual needs. From the inception of this initiative, the goal was to ensure that experienced-based learning opportunities offered critical business value and that it was aligned with not only HR learning strategies, but also with the company's business unit as well as overall strategies. After demonstrating that opportunities could be customized to accommodate flexibility in time for employee participation, business units were receptive to making it part of their career development offerings and built on the successes of the program.

Measuring Impact and Effectiveness

User feedback was monitored to gain insights into participation in the program, effectiveness of the program, application of learning, business results, employee satisfaction, and improvements to the program.

A strategy was designed to

- Determine readiness and awareness of the program, its perceived value by employees and managers, and how well it was being utilized by employees.
- Ascertain the business impact of the program, including employee satisfaction with the learning activities and application of learning on the job.
- Establish its impact on employee morale, retention, and performance.
- Evaluate financial impact, using criteria such as cost saving/avoidance, revenue growth, and increase in innovative solutions.
- Make recommendations for continuous improvement of the initiative.

Information is reported to senior management on a periodic basis and includes "hits" to the program-specific website, how many new participants the program has been deployed to, number of posted and available opportunities in the learning opportunity bank, and number of filled postings—or matches of opportunity to employee need. Feedback forms are sent 30 days following the completion of the activity to determine satisfaction levels and application to the job (Levels 1 and 3 measurements).

An example of the initial business impact of the program, shown in Table 9.3, is found in the results of an application and impact study conducted in 2Q 2007.

Table 9.3 Business Impact Comparison

	Employees		Managers	
	% Found Valuable	Average Rating	% Found Valuable	Average Rating
2006	93%	4.6	100%	4.6
2007	100%	5.0	80%	4.2

Survey and interview data were collected and analyzed for participants, including a representation of 35% managers and 65% nonmanagers. The findings indicated all interviewees (100%) viewed the program as a worthwhile investment for the company and should continue. Furthermore, when participants were asked to rate the value of the program to employee career development at the company, they stated that the program added value to both employees and the organization in the following ways:

- Skill development
- Networking
- "Larger picture" of the company
- Employee motivation
- Safe exploration of new roles
- Employee retention
- Employee productivity

Global Mentoring Program

In Chapter 8, we described IBM's mentoring program. In 2004, IBM "re-invented" its mentoring program, a blended approach to mentoring that provides diverse and just-in-time solutions that leverage multiple forms of technology and learning tools. The IBM mentoring program is designed to provide another avenue to help employees achieve their career goals, assist employees in the development of a network to stay connected in a remote environment, and to develop employees by providing an avenue for skills and knowledge growth.

The program's multimedia strategy allows mentoring to take place across different geographies, time zones, and cultures by selecting from a cafeteria of blended learning methods that best support their specific needs.

Infrastructure and Tools for Mentoring

In its re-invented form, the global mentoring program includes the following elements:

- A global corporate online employee directory was updated in late 2008 to enable employees to register as mentors or to find mentors anywhere across IBM's global enterprise.

- A "Dear Mentor" electronic forum was developed so employees across the globe could ask questions and receive responses from volunteer mentors within 24 hours.
- Centralized, web-based tools were developed to provide a one-stop mentoring guidance repository.
- Virtual technology such as Second Life and Metaverse was used to connect employees across geographies.
- Lunch and learn sessions, pod casts, webcasts, Wikis, and teleconferences were made available and accessible.

The company developed, implemented, and evaluated a blended learning approach to make mentoring pervasive in IBM, to fit the learning needs of the diverse populations in IBM, and to respond to changes in the global marketplace.

Focus Group Comments

A high-level summary of results from North American focus groups conducted in 2008 showed positive comments and trends in various categories, as is reflected in Table 9.4.

Table 9.4 Feedback from Focus Groups

Category	Feedback on Effects of Mentoring in IBM
New Hires/Retention	Employees are more aware of mentoring; more mentoring taking place within the company; mentoring helps promote climate of sharing; good for new hires.
Goal setting	The company's development plan, which includes a tool that enables employees to document their career plans including mentoring, provides a good link to mentoring; it helps to improve the quality of discussions with employees and helps set annual goals.
Recognition	Recognition programs are being utilized by employees as a way to say "thank you" to their mentors and peers. There is strong satisfaction when managers see mentees close skill gaps, increase knowledge, and excel at their jobs.
Management Support	Helps develop skills and learn in a nonthreatening environment. Helps managers increase the professional development of their employees without impacting their education budgets.

Table 9.4 Feedback from Focus Groups

Category	Feedback on Effects of Mentoring in IBM
Certification	Some jobs require certification in a variety of areas. Mentoring helps simplify the way for candidates to be certified with the assistance and support of the mentor in growing the right skills required for certification. Mentoring builds morale/very valuable; fabulous assistance in career development; sharpens leadership, technical and coaching skills for mentors.
Diversity (generational, cultural, age)	Mentoring considers different styles/roles; helps to get different perspectives outside current role/organization. "Helps an employee not only to fish but to know where the fish are!"
Tools	Great idea to use the corporate online employee directory as a global tool; mentoring website is a good central repository of information. Great response—mentoring website has had over 300,000 hits in the last four years.

Survey Results with Mentoring

Cross-geographic mentoring programs matched mentors from the United States with mentees from emerging countries, to focus on areas of development including

- Career progression and development
- Viewing the career path from different perspectives
- Patent development
- Personnel management
- Challenges faced working in different time zones
- Work/life balance
- Industry knowledge and research capabilities
- Navigating the company
- Developing global leadership skills and global business acumen

While several cross-geography mentoring programs were run in 2008, the following is one example of the program's effectiveness. In August 2008, employees in China were surveyed about the impact of cross-geographical mentoring by U.S.-based employees. The results are summarized in Table 9.5.

Table 9.5 Impact

Would use and/or recommend mentoring program to coworkers.	96%
Mentoring program brought great value to IBM.	96%
Mentors offered relevant and applicable information to mentees.	94%
Knowledge and awareness of different cultures was very important to their mentoring relationships.	91%

Collective Measurement of Career Development Programs at IBM

The collective impact of the combined career development initiatives are measured on a regular basis. A comprehensive measurement and evaluation plan has been put in place, where stakeholders are involved in setting standards and determining the indicators of success for the entire array of offerings. Employees as well as managers are asked what they would view as critical success factors for career development. A statistically representative sampling of managers and employee focus groups generated the criteria for success that allowed IBM to create a management system and culture that supports skill development and growth and gives employees the opportunity to improve skills and expertise.

Measurements are put into place at the learning activity and program level; however, how does a company evaluate the collective impact of all the various programs and activities? While each event or activity might be an isolated incident, often it's the collection of these items that provide the real value to employees—and the company.

One way IBM measures the overall impact of its collective career development programs is by using an employee survey that is conducted several times a year across random samples of the entire workforce. The purpose of the survey extends way beyond just measuring the impact of career development; it captures data related to job satisfaction, productivity, and other related areas. One of the questions that HR uses to gauge the impact of its career development efforts is one focused on career opportunities. This question is as follows: "I am given a real opportunity to improve my skills at IBM." Between 2003 and the first quarter of 2009, there was a 7-point gain in the response to this career-related question. This shows a significant increase in employee satisfaction in their perception of being able to improve their skills at IBM. While many factors could have contributed to the increase (or decrease) in responses to the employee survey questions, various new or re-vamped career development programs, processes, and tools in IBM were launched between 2003 and the end of 2008 that collectively may have had an impact on employees' perceptions of this career-related question.

Career Development: The Difference It Can Make

Perhaps you thought career development was a rather uncomplicated, straightforward process. People get a job, they do it, become proficient at it, and sometimes a promotion or new job opportunity comes along. However, after reading this book, you should be convinced that career development is more than just the job. It's about employees seeking their passions, finding meaning in their work, planning the best way to develop themselves, and finding the right learning activities to develop expertise. It's also about enabling the company to achieve organizational goals and ultimately provide value to the client.

The past eight chapters of this book have been dedicated to exploring the components of an agile career development process and providing examples of best practices that have proven to be instrumental in creating an environment for employees to become engaged and meet their career milestones. It is important to view all the various components as a holistic system, whereby the output of one part of the process provides an input to the next part of the process. The career development journey begins from the moment the employee interviews for the job. Companies need to be mindful of setting employee expectations from the beginning so that employees have a view of the opportunities the company could offer them—and so that the company hires the right individuals who can close whatever skill gaps exist.

Once employees enter the company, they need to feel welcomed, and they need a plan for getting quickly immersed in the work they were hired to do. An appropriate on-boarding process and new employee orientation program can help employees get through any initial hurdles they may encounter to becoming productive in a timely fashion.

Additionally, introducing them to the career development process early in their tenure helps them to visualize the career possibilities so they can work with their managers on laying out plans for achieving career goals.

Companies need to consider how they are going to determine the types of job roles needed; the expertise required to fulfill those roles; and then how employees can gain the appropriate experiences and engage in various learning activities to progress in their careers. Instrumental to this is the creation of some form of common language or "taxonomy" for how jobs and associated skills are defined, how skills can be assessed to determine gaps, and how employees can identify the right learning activities and experiences needed to fulfill those roles. And learning activities can take many different forms, from the more traditional, such as classroom training or e-learning, to the more experiential, such as mentoring, job shadowing, stretch assignments, and job rotations. Companies need to provide a way to identify such activities—and create the environment that enables employees to engage in them.

It is also important for companies to create a career framework that gives employees a view of how to succeed in one or more career paths to gain depth and breadth of the expertise needed to succeed. The framework should be flexible enough to allow employees to move vertically along one career path, gaining different experiences in related job roles that build deep levels of expertise. Also important is to allow employees, over the course of several career paths, to grow a variety of skills and capabilities, gain experience, and become very versatile in several major areas. Building this type of individual capability helps to grow organizational capability that ensures companies have a workforce with the right expertise to provide the right value to clients.

All of these various aspects of a career development process need to come together for employees through a career development plan. The plan is a way for employees to think about what learning activities and experiences might be needed for them to become more skilled in their current roles or what their next career moves might be. Equally important is manager engagement in the discussion with employees on their development. Managers are the critical link of the support system that employees need to succeed. Managers have a responsibility to help their employees plan their development, as well as creating the right environment so they can execute their plans.

Lastly, companies must put in place the right measurement systems that continually gather feedback from employees, managers, executives, and clients to ensure that the career development process and associated programs are appropriate. At the time of this writing, continued changes in the global economy and rising unemployment, coupled with continued generational difference and the rapid changes in the way employees learn and gain knowledge, may have a profound impact on how career development is viewed in the future. Companies need to continually assess, measure, and change their career processes, programs, and tools to reflect the needs of their employees and their organizations.

The lessons provided in this book can guide companies on establishing the basics of career development, and if implemented, can help companies weather changes to make certain that employees have the appropriate expertise needed to ensure the future success of the company.

Endnotes

[1]Bing, Diana, and Dave Gettles. "Business Coaching and Executive Onboarding" presentation, July 2002.

[2]Phillips, Jack, J., editor. *In Action: Performance and Analysis Consulting* (Alexandria, VA: American Society for Training and Development, 2000), pp. 53–66.

[3]Downey, Diane and Tom March. "Comfortable Fit: Assimilating New Leaders," *Executive Talent*, Summer 2000.

[4]Downey, Diane, Tom March, and Adena Berkman. *Assimilating New Leaders: The Key to Executive Retention* (New York: AMACOM, 2001).

[5]Cappelli, Peter, "A Market-Driven Approach to Retaining Talent," *Harvard Business Review* (Jan/Feb 2000): pp. 103–111.

[6]Elsdon, Ron and Seema Iyer. "Measuring the Impact of Career Development on an Organization," Sun Microsystems Inc., 2000, p. 11.

[7]Kirkpatrick, Donald L. *Evaluating Training Programs: The Four Levels, 2nd Edition* (San Francisco: Berrett-Koehler Publishers, 1998).

[8]Phillips, Jack J. and Ron Drew Stone. *How To Measure Training Results: A Practical Guide to Tracking the Six Key Indicators* (New York: McGraw-Hill, 2002) p. 10.

[9]"Productivity Dynamics," *Your IBM Learning Continuum* (September 2003): p. 122.

[10]Elsdon, Ron and Seema Iyer. "Measuring the Impact of Career Development on an Organization," Sun Microsystems Inc., 2000, p. 18.

[11]Ibid.

[12]Weldon, Laverne. Adapted from IBM Document on Measurement Philosophy, 2007.

[13]"Productivity Dynamics," *Your IBM Learning Continuum* (September 2003).

[14]Valencius, Matt. Adapted from IBM Document, Global Sales School, 2009.

[15]Interview with Matt Valencius, Executive with the Center for Advanced Learning, IBM, April 6, 2009.

[16]Ibid.

Index

D

E

H

I

P

Q

R

S

T

U

V

W-X

Y-Z